# The Way
# of Goodness and Holiness

## A Spirituality for Pastoral Ministers

*Richard M. Gula, SS*

LITURGICAL PRESS
Collegeville, Minnesota

www.litpress.org

Cover design by David Manahan, OSB.

| 1 | 2 | 3 | 4 | 5 | 6 | 7 | 8 | 9 |
|---|---|---|---|---|---|---|---|---|

**Library of Congress Cataloging-in-Publication Data**

Gula, Richard M.
    The way of goodness and holiness : a spirituality for pastoral ministers / Richard M. Gula.
      p. cm.
    Includes bibliographical references (p.     ).
    ISBN 978-0-8146-3347-2 — ISBN 978-0-8146-3952-8 (e-book)
    1. Lay ministry—Catholic Church.    2. Spiritual life—Catholic Church. I. Title.

BX1920.G86 2011
248.4'82—dc22                            2010031569

"The title of this volume captures two of its dimensions: it defines *the way* to goodness and holiness with rich descriptions of thirteen virtues, and charts *the way* with suggested steps to foster each. Rooted in a trinitarian and christological vision, and using the framework of the components of formation familiar today (human, spiritual, intellectual, and pastoral), Richard Gula draws upon varied sources to enrich his exploration: Scripture (sometimes with fresh interpretations), tradition, and insights from literature, psychology, and contemporary writers from varied fields. With keen observations about contemporary cultural realities and psychological insight he realistically assesses the difficulties inherent in growing in virtue today. A valuable resource for those who wish to be more intentional about growth in goodness and holiness, and for those leading programs of formation for ministry."

— *Zeni Fox*
*Professor of Pastoral Theology*
*Seton Hall University*

"A key axiom of sound spirituality is: reflect, don't merely react. When we do this though, one of the results is an uncertainty that we may find disconcerting. However, it is at these very unstable moments in our life that we are given the opportunity to deepen spiritually and grow psychologically. Richard Gula in *The Way of Goodness and Holiness* helps us welcome these opportunities—not with ready-made answers but with wise guidance on how we can better live with these questions honestly and fruitfully. I like that kind of book."

— *Robert J. Wicks*
*Author of* Prayerfulness: Awakening
to the Fullness of Life
*Professor, Loyola University Maryland*

"What a splendid job Richard Gula has done in closing the gap between moral theology and spiritual theology. His key is the pursuit of virtue by which we become both good *and* holy. This book is of such importance that lay ministers, religious, and clergy—at whatever stage of formation or ongoing formation—will recognize that The *Way of Goodness and Holiness* is required reading. Indeed anyone who wants to understand how morality and spirituality inform one another should take note of Gula's extraordinary achievement."

— *Michael Downey*
*Editor,* The New Dictionary of
Catholic Spirituality

"Richard Gula's *The Way of Goodness and Holiness* could not be more timely. With clarity, insight, sensitivity, and a welcome straightforwardness, Gula deftly explores the fundamental qualities of character that anyone ministering in the church should embody. In a text that is eminently readable, refreshingly practical, and unusually wise, Gula shows why the most authentic and effective ministers are those in whom virtues such as gratitude, humility, generosity, compassion, and not least of all, humor, shine. Moreover, by integrating morality and spirituality, Gula reminds us that ministering well is both more fulfilling and more challenging than we customarily think, precisely because it is a call to ongoing conversion. This book is a gift and a summons for anyone engaged in ministry today."

> — *Paul J. Wadell*
> *Professor of Religious Studies*
> *St. Norbert College*
> *De Pere, Wisconsin*

"Father Richard Gula's book, *The Way of Goodness and Holiness*, is not a manual or how-to book of spirituality for pastoral ministers. Instead, he provokes the hearts and souls of pastoral ministers. He persuasively insists that they embrace fully the life in God that they proclaim and serve in others."

> — *Reverend Louis J. Cameli*
> *Cardinal's Delegate for Formation*
> *and Mission*
> *Archdiocese of Chicago*

"Christianity is not a set of doctrines, but a way of life. How that life may be nourished is the subject of Gula's book. A veteran ethicist, Father Gula combines the best insights of virtue ethics with classical Christian spirituality. This work will repay anyone who is serious about the one who says, 'I am the way.'"

> — *Lawrence S. Cunningham*
> *John A. O'Brien Professor of Theology*
> *The University of Notre Dame*

# Contents

### What Will Help Us along the Way?

# Introduction

Before you begin to read this book, stop here to do a short spiritual exercise. It's an examination of conscience and character much like the one I did that gave rise to the structure and content of this book. In this way, you will begin to write your own spirituality for pastoral ministry.

Imagine being at a recognition dinner held in your honor on the occasion of your retirement from ministry. How would longtime colleagues describe you? What stories from your ministry would they tell? What would be the dominant theme in the conversation among the guests about the sort of person you were with colleagues, families, children, and the people you served? Write down three virtues that you aspire to embody in ministry and that you hope would be noted in the speeches and conversations about you:

(1) _____ (2) _____ (3) _____

An exercise like this helps us to see how our spiritual life takes flesh. Examining who we are and who we want to become can affirm us in our growth and prompt us to become better. But we need more than to aspire to be better. We also need to set our sights on what we want as pastoral ministers. Why are we in ministry? Do we want a career as an ecclesiastical officer? Do we want to do a lot of things for people? Where do we want our life to go? If we don't know where we want to go, we will easily end up somewhere else. Being clear about where we are headed as pastoral ministers can keep alive the zeal we once knew upon entering ministry. Clarity of purpose can also bring needed strength or restore enthusiasm to sustain us through the drudgery of routine and the ambiguity of tough decisions.

The way to fulfillment in pastoral ministry, or "holiness" in spiritual terms, does not consist in great achievements or ecstatic mystical moments. Rather, it consists in how we live along the way and in how we deal with what is at hand in all its earthiness and in all its demands. To see fulfillment in how we live from day to day is different from the way contemporary society measures success and happiness. The alternative vision of fulfillment in this book asks, how can we be authentic wherever we are and in whatever happens, even when things do not turn out the way we plan? The way to fulfillment, or authentic holiness, in pastoral ministry is to follow the way of goodness expressed through the virtues.

*The Way of Goodness and Holiness* develops a morally integrated spirituality for pastoral ministers by reflecting on virtues. Turning to virtue as a way to express our spirituality enables us to bring together who we are with who we hope to become by means of how we respond to the challenges that face us. The virtues that I make central to this book are habits, or acquired dispositions, that enable us to be our best in mediating the love of God; in coping with the responsibilities, frustrations, and freedoms of pastoral ministry; and in fostering the mission of the church to be both a sign and an instrument of our union with God and of the unity of all humankind (LG 1). My aim is to discuss these virtues sufficiently so as to indicate what seems most important about them for pastoral ministers. Like any virtue, we develop the ones discussed in this book by observation, imitation, practice, and the responsible use of our freedom. We develop in virtue through the ways we respond not only to the ordinary, uneventful events of our life where the stakes aren't so high but also through the ways we meet challenges where situations are more tense and the consequences more significant.

My descriptions of the virtues are not portraits of any one person. I necessarily take aspects from various people to construct a composite of what the virtue entails. I identified these virtues largely by observing other ministers who seem to have been effective in their ministry, who have won the admiration and respect of the people they served, who seem to be about as happy as anyone can expect to find in this life, and who other pastoral ministers recognize as models of goodness and holiness. While I have never met a minister who embodies all of these virtues equally, I have met any number who live many of them quite admirably. In fact, the experience of writing this book, as I hope you may feel in reading it, was like walking in the shoes of these good and holy people.

This book can stand on its own or be read in tandem with my last book, *Just Ministry: A Professional Ethics for Pastoral Ministers* (Paulist Press, 2010). After giving workshops on material from that book, I received feedback telling me that the ethics material was good but incomplete. Some who heard me would say that they felt as though I had started a musical scale but did not finish it. The missing "ti" and "do" was spirituality. This book is an attempt to complete the scale by developing a morally integrated spirituality for pastoral ministers.

The conviction guiding this book is that we recognize our spirituality from the outside in. That is, we begin with how our spirituality manifests itself in our character traits and in our style of life. These external expressions are the public face of our spirituality. They make our spirituality inseparable from our moral identity expressed in virtues. Virtues help us to live and act well so that we might fulfill what God hopes for us by being made in the image of God and by being called to imitate Christ Jesus.

We are at an extraordinary time in the development of moral theology and spiritual theology. For too long, these two disciplines went their separate ways. One of the reasons for their divorce was that moral theology became too preoccupied with actions and left concern for the person to spiritual theology. That is changing now.

We are at a historical moment in the renewal in these two disciplines when the necessary interdependence of goodness and holiness is clearly visible. Spirituality is the wellspring of the moral life, and the moral life is the public face of our spirituality.

Furthermore, the spiritual and moral dimensions of life are about the quality of our relationships. Spirituality is fundamentally about our relationship to God, and morality is about keeping this relationship central by showing our love for God by living in right relationships with all that God has created. The moral journey begins in that spiritual space where we accept God's love for us and awaken to responsibility for promoting the well-being of persons and the community in harmony with the environment. Hence, spirituality and morality mutually influence each other.

A sign of authentic spirituality is the life it engenders. As the biblical criterion has it, "You will know them by their fruits" (Matt 7:20). Without spirituality, morality gets cut off from its roots in the experience of God and so loses its foundation in grace and its character as a personal response to God's love. Likewise, without morality, spirituality can spin off into an interior life of ethereal ideas that never become real. Then the criticism that spirituality is about some other life and some other world would be true. But spirituality permeates all aspects of morality. To reduce spirituality to the interior life apart from its public expression is to make it like an incomplete sentence. It lacks a predicate. Moreover, reducing spirituality to the interior life promotes a form of dualism that makes spirituality disembodied. But spirituality's desire to be in union with God and morality's quest to respond to all things so as to respond to God's action upon us include every aspect of life and pervade our whole identity—our convictions, feelings, perspective, intention, attitudes, and behavior. No facet of being a person or of living in relationship to others is untouched by spirituality and morality.

But this book is not about spirituality and morality in general. It is about the spirituality of pastoral ministers that expresses itself in the life of virtue. Precedent for such a project can be found in St. Paul's Pastoral Epistles, especially 1 Timothy 3, where we find his list of virtues that serve as qualifications for bishops and deacons. It can also be found in his list of virtues that indicate a life lived under the power of the Holy Spirit (Gal 5:22-23). While there is no canonical set of virtues to prescribe a ministerial spirituality, there are some virtues that so reflect the life of Christ that they would be fitting ways of being for anyone who assumes the role of a pastoral minister. If you did the opening spiritual exercise, then you have already named what you regard as core virtues of a morally integrated spirituality for pastoral ministry.

The structure of this book came from my own elaboration of this exercise. I thought about this project in the metaphor of a journey with a GPS device as my guide. "Begin at the end" is the wisdom of a GPS device. We need to type in where we are and where we are going if our device is to show us the way. So the first part of this book identifies the ends of our spiritual journey. Where are we going? We are becoming more fully human, more like Christ, more disciplined in expressing our faith, and more virtuous in living from day to day. The second part is how we get there. I elaborate on virtues that I think a spiritual GPS device would disclose as necessary if we are going to be effective and happy in seeking our spiritual goals. In ordering the virtues, I did not follow the classical division of cardinal virtues that are derived from a particular concept of human nature. Rather, my ordering follows the four areas of development in ministerial life familiar to formation personnel—human, spiritual, intellectual, and pastoral. These four areas provide the structure of ministerial formation programs and have been identified as such in the instruction given by Pope John Paul II in his March 25, 1992, post-synodal apostolic exhortation *Pastores Dabo Vobis* (42). My treatment of each virtue ends with suggested practices to nurture that virtue. While these are quite ordinary actions, my contention is that when they are done intentionally as ways of responding to God, they can become spiritual practices that both give praise and thanks to God as well as nurture the moral life with virtuous dispositions. For the conclusion, I describe what will help us to make this journey—community, friendship, mentors and models, and spiritual practices.

My hope is that this book will be a source of information, inspiration, and aspiration for everyone in ministry, the ordained and the non-ordained alike. This book provides information about necessary virtues for ministry and how one's spiritual life and moral life mutually influence one another. I hope it inspires by affirming, encouraging, and confirming the way so many in ministry have been responding to the Holy Spirit through the development of virtues. It can also be a source of aspiration by holding out new levels of goodness and holiness that we have yet to attain.

I also wrote this book with an eye toward the needs of ministerial formation personnel. I hope this book stimulates the reflection of those in formation on the set of virtues formators would want ministers to acquire in order to serve the needs of today's church and how formation communities might adapt in order to model and facilitate growth in virtue. While reading this book, ask yourself, "What's missing? What else needs to be included to develop each area?" By using the reflections in this book as a starting point and asking questions like these, formators can come to a shared understanding of the sort of character and behaviors they think best fit the demands of ministry today.

Just as moral character requires friends to be fully formed, so too does writing a book. I am fortunate to have such friends. They rose to the occasion again to help me bring this book to its final form. Susan Alexander and Sr. Maureen Hester, SNJM, read each chapter along the way and kept encouraging me during the most difficult part of this process. My Sulpician colleague, Fr. Philip S. Keane, along with my friends Frs. Ron Chochol and Dick Sparks, CSP, read the manuscript once completed and offered suggestions to make the book clearer. I thank them immensely. I am also grateful to all of my students in my professional ethics course and to the many ministers, clerical and lay, who have participated in my workshops and lectures on this subject. They have influenced my thinking more than they will ever know. With deep gratitude, I dedicate this book to the faculty, staff, and students of the Franciscan School of Theology of the Graduate Theological Union in Berkeley, California, where so many lives model the portrait of the virtuous minister I sketched in this book. They have shown me the way to goodness and holiness.

# Where Are We Going?

# 1

## The Spiritual Journey

The good news of Christian faith is that God's loving us in the Spirit is the first principle on which to build a spiritual and moral life. We are made out of love for love. Christian spirituality began with God giving us the Holy Spirit through the resurrection of Jesus. This Spirit is at work in every aspect of our life—our work, our leisure, our civic duties, our home life, and our pastoral ministry. We cannot induce the Spirit's presence or conjure it up. It is pure gift. Our task is to be attentive, receptive, and responsive. This chapter lays out four goals of our spiritual journey: becoming human, imitating Christ, practicing the faith, and developing virtues.

### Becoming Human

To be human is to be in relationship. We grow in goodness and holiness in and through the relationships that make up our lives. Our spiritual journey is fundamentally relational. The first and all-encompassing relationship is with God who is already in relationship with us, accepts us, and gives ultimate meaning and value to our lives. Because of the pervasive presence of God's Spirit, all life is lived in the presence of God and is responsive to God. We are inevitably involved with God and drawn to God in and through all things. As a result, the spiritual life is not about having extraordinary experiences, but it is about how we express in our everyday experiences

3

our relation to God and our relation with each other. No aspect of living escapes our spirituality. It is like the herb that flavors the sauce.

Living a spiritual life is about letting the power of being accepted by God work in and through all other relationships. From our foundational relationship to God, all other relationships fan out like concentric circles around the central core—God. How we relate to each other is just as important spiritually as how we relate to God. The qualities of character that we bring to everyday relationships are not separate from the spiritual life. They are its public face. The call to be good and to do what is right that arises from being in the presence of another is always spiritual at its roots as a call from God. It is no surprise then that the biblical witness makes the quality of our relationships the benchmark for measuring the authenticity of our spirituality (cf. Mark 12:29-31; Matt 25; and Gal 5:22-23).

Hence, we ought not to associate spirituality exclusively with its vertical dimension of worshiping God through devotional practices, such as those we often find and do in church. While a spiritual life must include such spiritual practices to show our love for God, the spiritual life is also intimately intertwined with our relationships with self, other people, and nature. Our spirituality shows itself in whether we live in harmony with our bodies or out of touch with them, in whether we are loving or bitter, in whether we give ourselves to God and to others in true self-forgetfulness or live only for ourselves, and in whether we care for the earth or pollute the environment. That is why we cannot limit the spiritual life to prayer or to interior movements aroused in prayer. Our spirituality manifests itself not only in religious practices or affections but also in a virtuous life. For this reason, it must encompass whatever living in right relationships requires of us.

The opposite of having a spiritual life is to be so isolated and drawn in on ourselves that we have neither the skills nor energy for life-giving relationships. That is what it means to lose one's soul. A healthy soul keeps us connected; it gives us the energy to go out of ourselves to love and to be loved, to know and to be known, to be free and to set free. This dynamic orientation of the self reflects one of the insights of Karl Rahner's vision of the person as "spirit-in-the-world." That is, we were made for relationship with God. To be dynamically oriented toward God constitutes the most radical meaning of what a human person is—fundamentally related to God—and this relationship is the way to human fulfillment.

The theological roots of being relational lie in the uniquely Christian understanding of God as Trinity. The central theme of Trinitarian theology is that God's nature is relational. God is a community of persons radically equal to each other and bonded in mutual self-giving and receiving of love. Since we believe that we are made in the image of God, we can infer that we are social by nature and made to share. Our very capacity for relationships is one way we are "like God." The Trinitarian doctrine implies that our relationships ultimately bind us to God, that we are called to create a community characterized by equality, mutuality, and reciprocal giving and receiving for the sake of the well-being of all, and that we are persons by virtue of our relationship to one another.

Simply put, then, to be is to be in relationship. We have a self insofar as we are related with others. To think of a person without thinking of being in relationship is to miss the meaning of being a person. To live in right relationship with all things is the good we long for. Such a view makes human relationships a privileged locus for experiencing God and authentic holiness a communal affair.

No wonder having the skills to develop and sustain life-giving relationships is a necessary requirement for anyone who becomes a candidate for pastoral ministry. Ministry is a relational profession. The development and quality of pastoral contacts depends a great deal on the minister's relational skills. For this reason, no one is fit for ministry who cannot relate—that is, who shows no signs of having sustained friendships, who is careless about boundaries, who is arrogant or quarrelsome, or whose style of relating is to control, intimidate, manipulate, demean, or shame. Pastoral ministry requires a person who is open to others, able to empathize, affable and non-defensive, flexible and collaborative. To be emotionally rigid, defensive, authoritarian, selfish, or dismissive of others would undermine the kind of relationships that would image God and mediate God's presence.

This relational view of the self is a necessary corrective to the Enlightenment view of the person that has had a far-reaching influence on Western spirituality and morality. The Enlightenment view of radical individualism thinks of the person as an individual first, not as a social being. The influence of this view on our morality and spirituality has been to make us too self-absorbed. In morality, it thinks too much about securing individual rights and liberties and not enough about what a just society is. Procedural justice (the fair enforcement of rules to protect individual interests) eclipses distributive justice (sharing resources so that all might flourish). In spirituality, this view thinks that we can discover the true self by turning inward and disengaging from others. It wants to make solitude prevail over community and introspection the primary tool of spiritual growth.

Understanding the self as fundamentally relational, however, has refocused our attention on the social character of being human. As my African colleagues put it, "I am because we are." As personalist philosophers would have it, "we is prior to I." Personal identity derives from social identity. Once we accept ourselves as existing in a web of interdependent relationships, then we can appreciate how personal flourishing is always entwined with the flourishing of others, including the earth. There is no self-realization apart from responsibility for our neighbors and for the earth. Humanness and relationality are proportional to one another. We realize our humanness to the extent that we choose to be related. A deeper participation in the human community enhances the humanity of each person, while the failure to establish community diminishes the humanity of all. We discover ourselves not by retreating into solitude to escape social responsibility, but by being drawn into the lives of others and learning about ourselves from social interaction. That makes it possible to say that the moral and spiritual life are measured by the quality of our relationships.

The focus on the relational dimension of being human has redirected spiritual theology from an overemphasis on the interior life to recognizing the centrality of being in right relationship with others. Michael Downey correctly notes that the turn to relationships for understanding the self naturally connects our spirituality to the moral demands of creating a new social order based on mutuality, equality, and reciprocity rather than on domination and submission. A morally integrated spirituality requires nurturing virtues that strengthen our relational bonds, such as the virtues of gratitude, fidelity, compassion, generosity, and justice. Spiritual practices within this spirituality contribute toward establishing rightly ordered relationships with God, the wider human community, and with the environment.[1]

That we must relate to others is inevitable. How we relate is a matter of character and choice. Morality pertains to our responsibility for the relationships that constitute our lives. Responding to God is a daily choice. We hear the call of God and respond to it in the relationships that make up our lives. James Keenan has argued that we are relational in three ways: generally, specifically, and uniquely. Each correlates with a cardinal virtue. As relational beings in general, we need justice; our specific relationships call us to fidelity; the unique relationship we have with ourselves calls us to self-care. Living in response to God requires prudential discernment of what constitutes the just, faithful, and self-caring way of life we ought to follow.[2] Choosing to be virtuous through repeated actions allows us to become the person God has called us to be. Becoming good by following the way of virtue is integral to becoming holy.

Our quest for God in the spiritual life must be consistent with our human nature. Since we are relational persons, our spirituality must extend beyond ourselves and our interior life to include a communal dimension. As relational persons, we are bound together in a shared life where we are responsible to each other in mutual support and challenge. Living interdependently is part of what it means to be church. As church, we no longer live for ourselves but are mutually accountable to one another for our character and virtue. To make spirituality a private affair between me and God or to make the spiritual life something done in solitary isolation would be rejecting not only part of our nature but also our calling as the People of God.

In short, Christian spirituality is a cooperative adventure. It is ultimately communitarian, requiring enduring relationships with people of faith who share common practices, spiritual and moral, and stable convictions about who God is and who we ought to become as disciples of Jesus. The church is where we gather around the person of Christ and learn to live in his spirit. To Christ and his spirit, we turn next.

## Imitating Christ

We do not form in isolation the fundamental attitudes that shape our way of being in the world. We come to them by imitating others. One of the most important decisions we will have to make is whom we will imitate. Christians find in Jesus the Christ the one most worth imitating. He is for us the fully human response to the experience of God's love. Because Jesus reveals the fullness of what is human by realizing it in himself, he is for believers the exemplar of what life is like when lived with God as the ultimate object of our loyalty.

Through Jesus we learn a great deal about what being a good human person is. As such, he is for us the paradigmatic character for the virtuous life. For pastoral ministers, he is the constant point of reference to the question, "Who am I called to be?" because being conformed to the image of Christ as a disciple is the kind of life every pastoral minister strives to embody. The long tradition of *imitatio Christi* echoes with virtues. The moral imperative for us is not simply "be good" but "be good the way Jesus was." Or, to put it in the Pauline idiom, "Let the same mind be in you that was in Christ Jesus" (Phil 2:5).

That Jesus ought to be the guiding pattern for our lives is set forth in John 13:34, perhaps our most succinct statement of New Testament ethics: "Just as I have loved you, you also should love one another." Hence, Christian spirituality requires discipleship. In the moral imagination, "as" links our interests in character and virtue to the paradigmatic life of Christ. If we are to be disciples today and live faithful to Jesus, then our character and actions ought to resemble, rhyme with, or harmonize with the pattern we find in his story. The challenge for living as a disciple of Jesus today can be understood in two terms: faithful and creative. That is, we are to be faithful to the Jesus revealed in the New Testament and mediated by the church, and we are to be creative in our response to the challenges of life today.

But how do we cross over from the life of Jesus to our own? We do it by means of analogical reflection.[3] As William Spohn explains, analogy is the way we learn. Through analogies, we grasp what is new by comparing it to what we already know. For example, my analogy for structuring this book as a moral and spiritual journey is using a GPS device to plan a road trip. Another example comes from the world of health care. Our decision to withdraw the ventilator from a patient with terminal lung cancer is analogous to deciding to withdraw dialysis from a patient with end-stage kidney disease. In everyday living, the analogy to showing compassion by stopping to assist at an accident along the highway is the Samaritan giving aid to the victim who fell among robbers along the road. Without analogies, we have no bridge from what we know to what is not yet clear. Analogical reflection on the gospels tries to imagine actions that are appropriate to our present situation and faithful to the story of Jesus. As Spohn concludes, "The new actions will be analogical because they will be partly the same, partly different, but basically similar to the relevant portion of the story of Jesus. . . . Something is found in the story of Jesus that can be exemplary and paradigmatic for how to act today."[4]

Analogical reflection is how we cross over from the historical and social context of the time of Jesus to our own. Discipleship today cannot mean simply accepting literally every command of Jesus, nor can it mean reproducing the externals of his life as if we were invited to an exercise of nostalgia. Because we do not live when Jesus did and because he did not face the challenges that we do, we should not try to copy the external aspects of his life point for point. Imitation is not mimicry. Mimicry forgets that the strategies and responses of Jesus were based on the developmental influences of his own life and the resources he had available as a Jewish man in first-century Palestine.

For example, just because Jesus died at the hands of the political and religious leaders of his day does not mean that we ought to be martyred in similar fashion. That Jesus drove the money changers out of the temple does not mean that the church ought to have no dealings with money. That Jesus invited women into his inner circle or welcomed children and touched them does not mean that we are free to relate to others without regard for appropriate boundaries. Trying to transpose into our own day everything that Jesus did is anachronistic and reductive. Jesus is our paradigm, not a blueprint to copy point for point. To do so would confuse mimicry for imitation, and that would be the death of any creative response to new issues and a new era.

The question of discipleship is not to approach every responsibility or to answer every moral question in terms of WWJD?: "What would Jesus do?" Although well-intentioned, that question too easily opens the way to fundamentalistic mimicry. The challenging question for us is "How can we be as faithful to God in our day as Jesus was in his?" Of course, we cannot deduce faithful behavior from a particular command or deed of Jesus by strict logic. We can, however, use the stories of Jesus as our primary examples of fidelity. We can discover the fitting response to our situation by moving analogously from the story of Jesus to the demands of our own life.

Following Jesus today, then, is not a matter of simply repeating the externals of his life. But it is the matter of striving to make his wisdom, his spirit, and his dispositions toward life shape our own. Authentic imitation is making our life rhyme with his. We interpret our lives in "the light of Christ" by using the words, deeds, and stories of Jesus and about Jesus as our primary reference point for informing our response. Each of our lives, then, is a variation on his. Our own variation is creative yet faithful when we can spot the rhyme between the gospels' witness to Jesus and the moral demands of the moment. Both faithful attention to what we have received from the gospel and creative openness to what is at hand are the moral performances of analogical reflection.[5]

Imaginatively engaging a collage of gospel stories gives us a picture of what the spirit of Jesus is like and who we might become in imitation of his freedom and his faithfulness. Jesus lived with his heart set on one thing—the reign of God's love. The secret of his being able to live a life of nonviolent resolution of conflict and inclusive, self-giving love was that he accepted himself as being accepted by God. The pivotal event in his life for experiencing God's acceptance, I believe, was his baptism in the Jordan when the voice spoke a blessing from the rip in the heavens: "You are my own dear Son. I am pleased with you" (Matt 3:17; Mark 1:9-11; Luke 3:21-22). To understand Jesus' attitude, freedom, and fidelity, it helps to imagine that throughout his life he felt the gaze of God's appreciation and kept hearing in his ears the blessing of those words received out of the waters of his baptism. These words of worth formed his consciousness. The rest of the gospels demonstrates the practical effect of holding fast to them. When Jesus looks on the poor, the hungry, the meek, and the marginalized, he sees them as blessed because he is hearing God's voice telling him that God is seeing him and the world that way. He drew from the treasure of this blessing in order to bless in turn.

John Shea tells a Sufi story that gets to the heart of Jesus' identity and capacity to bless. As the story goes, Jesus was on the road with his disciples when some people began to throw stones at him and to curse him. Jesus blessed them. His disciples were dumbfounded. "Why do you bless those who curse you?" they demanded to know. Jesus said, "I can only give what I have in my purse."[6]

Shea goes on to comment that because Jesus was secure in his being blessed by God, he knew where his treasure lay. When we are not so sure of being loved, a rock is always close at hand. When we start to throw rocks of curse or condemnation, it is because we can't find our purse of blessings. But to live as a disciple is to live by our blessings and to let go of attachments and illusions to greatness that enslave us, such as the prideful desire for recognition to secure our worth, or the crippling fear of rejection for not being worthy of love, or a slavish conformity to what everyone else seems to be doing or thinking.

To be a disciple demands the freedom to let go of self-made securities that preoccupy our hearts so that we have room for divine love. Because Jesus knew whose he was, he did not have to latch on to false loves in order to secure his identity. Discipleship begins with letting go. By following the way of renunciation (Mark 8:34), we can rest secure in God's loving us. So we have to let go of attachments that enslave us, such as our attachment to position, power, or prestige that secure our worth, or to our reliance on obeying the laws or saying our prayers as ways to save us. Until we can give up the presumption that we can insure our lives by creating these surrogate loves, we are not ready for discipleship.

Perhaps the most challenging of gospel stories calling us to the radical renunciation of discipleship is the story of the rich young man (Matt 19:16-30). The young man asks Jesus what he must do to share in everlasting life. Jesus tells him to keep the commandments. The young man says he has kept them all his life. But being a law-abiding citizen does not make for discipleship. Jesus invites the young man to give up his surrogate loves—all those things he relied on for status, security, worth, and well-being—and to follow Jesus. The young man went away sad for he relied on much.

What is it about the rich young man that makes it impossible for him to share fully in divine love? We get a hint from a Peanuts cartoon that finds Linus sharing his hopes with Charlie Brown. Linus says, "So I've decided to be a very rich and famous person who doesn't really care about money, and who is very humble but who still makes a lot of money and is very famous, but is very humble and rich and famous." Charlie looks at him in amazement and says, "Good luck." Charlie has it exactly right: "Good luck" if you try to live with a heart set on more than one thing. What makes being a disciple difficult for the rich young man is that he wants to hang on to his homemade securities as the source of his worth and loveableness. Jesus invites him to let go so that his heart can be filled with divine love. Jesus invites us to do likewise.

Jesus' singular work was to do what he experienced God calling him to do—set people free and invite them into communion with God and with one another. His miracles, for example, are works of liberation that enabled the people who were healed to go back into society and enjoy companionship and other life-giving relationships. His parables are judgments on the use of power to exclude people from an inclusive community. Jesus was free enough in himself so that he could include a great variety of people despite the features that marginalized them as outcasts. If we are to be disciples in the spirit of Jesus, then we must do likewise—be free enough in ourselves to nurture moral sensitivities that watch out for those who are hurt or lost, that make room for the stranger and those on the margins of society, that are disposed toward mercy and forgiveness, that seek the nonviolent resolution of conflict, and that challenge any striving for superiority over another.

While Jesus did not leave a detailed program of action that we are to follow as disciples, he did leave a vision of God's dream for us—the reign of God.[7] His hearers already knew about other kingdoms—Herod and Caesar had already made their mark on them. The reign of God is what the world will look like when God reigns and not Caesar. The reign of God is the equivalent of the presence of God—a pure grace to be discovered like a treasure hidden in a field (Matt 13:44-46); hence, not a natural right, nor something to be merited.

Jesus saw the reign of divine love as embracing all humanity. He conferred upon it an added intensity by honoring through his teaching and his witness the basic equality of each person freed from the tight social boundaries of nationality, race, gender, or religion. For example, Jesus did not exclude sinners from his company, as did the Pharisees. Even prostitutes and tax collectors were welcome at his table. Salvation did not mean condemning sinners from afar, but going forth to meet them and offer them a way out of their sin by building new relationships. Nor did Jesus exclude the crippled, the infirm, the possessed, or the unclean, as did the Essenes. Nor did he exclude the poor and needy, as did the Sadducees. Jesus did not fear approaching these people because he was motivated by divine love to touch and to heal them. While the society of his time regarded women and children as defenseless property, Jesus did not exclude women from his company of intimate friends, nor did he bar children from his presence. Rather, he championed them as witnesses to the reign of God.

Jesus showed concretely what life in the Spirit looks like, as he imitated his Father's love in transcending all forms of particularism and exclusivism. In contrast to the world of his day marked by sharp social boundaries, Jesus reflected an alternative social vision. He did not preach about how to be good within a dominating system. His preaching and his life radically challenged the dominating structures and practices of his day. He made inclusiveness the basic value for anyone who would be identified with him and his mission. From Jesus we learn that the criterion for discipleship is to be able to make room in our hearts for everyone, and especially to be ready to stand on the side of those who are weakened by oppression of any sort.[8]

Jesus modeled what expanding our circle of inclusive love would look like by the way he interpreted the meaning and use of power, an issue that everyone in pastoral ministry needs to address. Jesus' understanding and use of power stands in contrast to the way officials of society and religion at that time were conceiving and exercising it. Jesus did not distrust power as such, but he conceived of it as a way to mediate divine love through service that liberates and unites and not as a force that dominates and devours the vulnerable (cf. Mark 10:29-42; Matt 20:25-28; Luke 22:25-27).

That this was such a new teaching for his disciples is evident in how they and the religious leaders of that time often served as foils to Jesus' loving use of power. Jesus refashions the disciples' imagination with new images of power and human relationships in the conflict between Peter and Jesus over forgiveness (Matt 18:21-35). "How many times must I forgive?" Peter asks Jesus. The contrast of Peter's "seven times" with Jesus' answer of "seventy times seven times" is more than a contrast between a definite number and an infinite capacity. It is a reversal in an image of power and superiority. Peter has the keys. So when he asks about the number of times he has to forgive, he is subtly asking Jesus when he can exercise his power to lock some out and others in. Jesus challenges his understanding of power and human relationships with an image of inclusion. Power that flows from the experience of divine love is not for keeping people inferior and distant but for creating a hospitable space where others can come in and be friends.[9]

In the same vein, Jesus instructs his disciples to avoid all known techniques that would secure positions of superiority in their social structure. They were not to use religious dress (to broaden their phylacteries or to lengthen their tassels) in order to attract attention. Nor were they to take the reserved seats in religious assemblies, which symbolized superior roles in the community. They were not to use titles, such as "rabbi," "father," or "master," which require others to recognize one's superior status (Matt 23:5-10). In short, they were not to dominate in the name of service.

Then there is the conflict between Jesus and his disciples who return to him after meeting a man casting out demons in Jesus' name (Mark 9:38-40; Luke 9:49-50). The disciples want to stop him. Why? He is not one of them. Jesus, however, does not want to stop him. Jesus has a different vision of who is "with them." "Whoever is not against us is for us," says Jesus. His priority is that people be free and brought under the reign of love. He tells them, in effect, unless people exhibit hostility toward you, assume they are your allies. It is not your role to exclude; people will exclude themselves by their attitude and behavior.[10]

This story shows how much the desire to be great, to be in control with power over others, can influence how we evaluate all the events of our life. In this instance the disciples are so self-absorbed in their desire for greatness that they hoard what is most important—the power to set people free. Their consciousness is so competitive that they are threatened by someone poaching on their territory. The fact that a man now lives free of demons is insignificant to them. What matters is that they did not work the wonder. They hold the power as the official exorcists, and they are fixed on guarding their turf. This stranger threatens to steal their importance. The disciples want to use their power to control the good and to make themselves great. The power in Jesus directed by divine love does not want to usurp the good, but the arrogant power in the disciples that wants to remain superior does.

When we strive for greatness, we weigh everything in terms of whether it promotes or diminishes us. Remember, in his purse Jesus carries only blessings. His whole disposition is to bless and not to curse, to forgive and not to seek revenge, to liberate and not to oppress. Jesus deliberately espouses a lifestyle of service and inclusiveness. But his disciples still want to exercise their power to control and exclude, as in Luke 9:51-56. Jesus commits himself to go to Jerusalem, the place of his suffering, and sends his disciples ahead to prepare people to welcome him and to preach the news of the reign of God. But a Samaritan village refuses to offer hospitality. Its refusal triggers a plan for retaliation in James and John. They react to rejection with rejection on steroids: "Do you want us to command fire to come down from heaven and consume them?" Jesus rebukes their passion for revenge and their scorched-earth policy. Jesus says, in effect, "Let's find a more welcoming village." The disciples want to use their power to get revenge; Jesus uses his to find another opportunity.[11]

Jesus' liberating power is also at work in the scene of healing the bent-over woman in Luke 13:10-17. In this scene, Jesus calls to a woman who has been bent over by an evil spirit for eighteen years. He places his hands on her, and she stands up straight. She who was once weak is now strong. Friends of Jesus rejoice over her liberation, but the officials of the synagogue who observe this are angry about what was done and when it was done. The power that liberates by making the weak strong is too challenging to the officials. Arrogant power of superiority wants to control the good by keeping some weak while others remain strong. The power that Jesus expresses is the power that transforms the structures of domination in the community.[12]

The great reversal of structures of power that Jesus reveals is especially evident in the famous conflict between Jesus and Peter in the footwashing scene in the Gospel of John 13:6-10. Sandra Schneiders's interpretation is especially insightful in giving us a portrait of a disciple.[13] In this scene, when Peter sees Jesus, the master, acting like a servant, he knows something new is afoot. This is not the picture Peter has in his imagination of the structure of relationships in the community. Peter realizes that, if he were to comply with the washing, he would be accepting a radical change in the way he ought to relate to others. The action of Jesus is challenging in a radical way the structure that makes some superior while others remain inferior. Such a conversion is more than Peter is willing to undergo. When Jesus deliberately reverses social positions by becoming the servant, he witnesses to a new order of relationships in the community and to a style of being a disciple wherein the desire to dominate has no place. When Peter finally allows himself to be washed, he accepts the call that discipleship is for service and not for domination.

Finally there is the cross and resurrection. The cross stands as the icon of Christianity not only because it is a symbol of self-sacrifice but also because it is the summary of the freedom and faithfulness that marked Jesus' life. Before the cross, Jesus emptied himself for the sake of others. On the cross, he is most empty of what he could do for himself. In the crucifixion, the power of domination is raging out of control. On the cross, Jesus does not resort to legions of angels to destroy the evil of those who appear to be in power. If he did, then his kind of power and theirs would be the same. The only difference would be in the size of the muscle. Jesus resorts to the only kind of power he knows—inclusive, liberating love—and offers forgiveness. The cross ultimately reveals the emptiness of oppressive power that devours the weak.[14] The passion and death of Jesus reveal the steadfast love of God unmasking the arrogance of power that nailed him up. The same steadfast love invites disciples of all ages to live as Jesus did—trusting in the power of divine love to sustain us.

The resurrection affirms that the way of Jesus is a truthful expression of living under the reign of God. Where Jesus has gone, we are bound to follow if we catch his spirit. If we are to be disciples in his spirit, then we must be free enough to nurture in ourselves moral sensitivities that have a special concern for those who are hurt or lost, that make room for the stranger and the outcast, that are disposed to act toward others with mercy and forgiveness, and that are inclusive of all. Because of the resurrection we can take the risk to be free and faithful as Jesus was.

But we cannot become disciples on our own. While it requires a commitment of faith for sure, discipleship also requires strong bonds of solidarity with others who share in the vision and mission of Jesus and pledge to be faithful to it. This is the role of the church in becoming disciples. Social scientists tell us that the metaphors we live by are largely caught by participating in the rituals and symbols of communities that live by them.[15] So, to remain committed to discipleship, we need not only the scriptural texts that reveal Jesus to us, but also the community that remembers him. We need a communal tradition of reflecting on Jesus' life and of living in imitation of him.

We need to live with people who can demonstrate that violence is not inevitable, that living in harmony with the earth is possible, that selfishness can be overcome by generosity, and that care and kindness are ways to call people to life. The imitation of Christ is a cooperative adventure. We need to be in relationship with people who challenge us to stay focused on what is true about being committed to witnessing to the reign of divine love. And we need people who love us enough to free us to be our true selves, and we need not fear taking risks on our own giftedness and that of others. This is what the church ought to be—a community of prophets and cheerleaders inspired by the life of Christ.

But even within a community like this, many of us may feel that being free and faithful in the way of Jesus is beyond our reach. Fair enough. So we need to be modest in our claims of faithful imitation. The words of Mother Emmanuel, head of the Carmelite monastery in Mark Salzman's novel, *Lying Awake*, could be words addressed to us: "No matter how many times we hear what it costs to follow Christ, we're still shocked when the bill comes, and we wonder all over again if we can pay it."[16] Our incapacity to pay the cost of discipleship only reminds us that we are works in progress. We are always letting go and learning to love with a more inclusive love.

Each of us will live as a disciple in a way that corresponds to our capacities and to our openness to the Holy Spirit. Jesus has shown us the way by being free and faithful to God through his inclusive love and liberating use of power. But the details are now left to us. We must figure out from his example and our capacity how we can become a sign and instrument of inclusive love. In the end, we have to think analogically how to love as we have been loved so that we will witness to the vision of Jesus that brings all peoples under the inclusive reign of divine love. Spiritual practices are the place and opportunities to open ourselves to the transforming power of divine love, and to encounter Christ and his call to discipleship.

## Practicing the Faith

The imagination's capacity to spot analogies in the stories of Jesus comes from grounding ourselves in Jesus' way of life. We can ground ourselves in Jesus through the regular exercise of devotional disciplines or spiritual practices. As William Spohn reminds us, "The practices of spirituality sharpen the Christian's capacities to discern what is appropriate. They ground the person in a way of life by shaping perception and moral dispositions. At the same time, the doctrines of the faith and its moral principles also set parameters for analogical imagination."[17] As we deepen our familiarity with Jesus and let that same mind be in us that was in Christ Jesus (Phil 2:5) through our spiritual practices, we can become more skilled at discerning who God is calling us to be and how God is calling us to live in accordance with the Gospel.

Common practices include the following, among others: the sacraments; reading and meditating on the Bible (*lectio divina*); praying the rosary; inspirational reading; making a retreat; fasting; eucharistic adoration (such as Benediction); novenas; reciting the Liturgy of the Hours (Divine Office); making the Stations of the Cross; using sacramentals like holy water, medals, and statues; singing hymns; making a pilgrimage to a holy site; making reparation; working for social justice; volunteering our service.

We do not engage in practices like these to conjure up the presence of God as though God were absent from us. In faith, we know that we are always living in the presence of God. Yet, in fact, we live in the world of ordinary experience and do not easily perceive the world of the Spirit. We are not always attentive to God's presence or conscious of responding to God in and through the way we respond to all things.

I once heard this story that captures the spirit of why we need a regular discipline of spiritual practices in our life. A young monk asked his abbot, "How can I be sure that I am in the presence of God?" The abbot replied, "You have as much control over that as you have the power to make the sun rise." In exasperation, the young monk exclaimed, "Then what use are all of our spiritual exercises?" To which the abbot replied, "You need your discipline of spiritual practices to make sure that you are paying attention when the sun does rise." We need some physical actions that intentionally focus our awareness of God loving us and addressing us, and we need intentional expressions of our loving God. Spiritual practices do that.

As physical ways to express our love for God, spiritual practices provide a space for God's Spirit to act on our soul. In this way they are "sacramental." As intentional, a spiritual practice is a deliberate, heartfelt effort to develop our awareness of God and love for God. An intentional practice is not an occasional burst of enthusiasm (I'm feeling pious today), nor a dutiful following of the law (the church requires it), nor a coerced caving in to social pressure (everyone is doing it). Rather, the practice as intentional is a personally committed exercise that we do on a regular basis and with an openness to be moved by the Spirit working in and through it, like going to Mass every Sunday or taking fifteen minutes of quiet every morning.

In addition to being physical and intentional, the other key term of reference to understand a spiritual practice is *God*. The practices' orientation to God helps us understand why we do them in the first place. We do them to open ourselves to God's love, to show our love for God, and to deepen our relationship with God. We do not do the practice in the first place to improve our health, to reduce our stress, to change our attitudes, or to reform our social relationships. The direct intention of the practice is to worship God, to show our love for God, to deepen our awareness of God, and to strengthen our relationship with God. Indirectly, however, there are morally formative effects that can come from doing the practice.

For example, praying with the gospel stories used in the previous section on discipleship may open us to our own attachments, exclusiveness, and misuse of power. Coming to such awareness under the influence of these stories may nurture the imagination with new images for becoming detached from our surrogate loves, for expanding our circle of inclusive love, and for being more liberating in our use of power. Cultivating our relationship to God through the spiritual practice of praying with gospel stories like this can be morally transforming when it helps us to see everything in relation to God and to our commitment to care about what God cares about in the way Jesus has shown us to care.

A strong note of caution must be sounded here about spiritual practices as morally transforming. The caution: nothing is automatic. There is no guarantee that if we do the practices then we will acquire a certain character or behave in a certain way. We must be careful about claiming too much for the transforming potential of doing spiritual practices. The connection between doing a practice and moral life is complex, not simple. While spiritual practices are necessary to keep alive our relationship to God and our way of seeing all things in relation to God, they are not sufficient for shaping moral behavior. We also need to make practical moral decisions and to develop virtuous habits in order to implement our spiritual relationship and vision. Moreover, since personal and cultural experiences are also at play in shaping our moral life, spiritual practices do not have a monopoly on the way we live. Given the many factors that influence the moral life, and given that not everyone engages religious devotions with the same depth of commitment, we cannot expect practices to ensure a virtuous life.

Nevertheless, spiritual practices do carry a rich potential for moral transformation when we engage them with the right intention and heartfelt commitment. One of the major aspects of the self subject to transformation by devotional practices is the imagination. The imagination is more important in our lives than we give it credit for, especially if we associate the imagination exclusively with fantasy and frivolity in an otherwise serious world. The imagination is much more than that. It is the bridge between spiritual practice and the moral life because its interpretive function makes sense of what life is all about and who we are. The imagination does this by seeing through images. Shaping the imagination is one of the central functions of spiritual practices in relation to a virtuous life. Christian spirituality believes that the images that come to us through the Christian story and rituals provide a truthful way of seeing the world. The more we participate in the stories, rituals, and language of our religious faith, the more likely we will form our character by its values and ways of seeing. Our devotional life is very much a part of the process by which we appropriate the images of the Christian story so that they shape our responses to all the relationships of our life.

Take our regular participation in the Eucharist as an example. Above all, worship is an act of loving God. We gather for eucharistic worship primarily to give thanks and praise to God for what God has done and continues to do for us in the Spirit of the risen Lord. We do not gather in order to derive moral imperatives or to become better persons. By gathering in faith, we put ourselves in the presence of God's Spirit and allow God to make a claim on us through ritual actions such as gathering as a community, breaking open the word, and sharing the one bread and the one cup at a common table. These ritual actions link us to morality by having a formative influence on our identity, perspective, and dispositions.

The influence on our identity comes from letting God have a claim on us in worship. Through worship, we define ourselves in relation to God and commit ourselves to what God cares about. Our religious identity can then serve as a critical alternative to any other relationship we might have or attachments we might acquire in the course of living out our responsibilities.

The influence on our perspective comes by participating in ritual actions filled with images that have the power to illuminate the meaning and direction of our lives. While the Eucharist is primarily about giving praise and thanks to God, it simultaneously trains us in how to see from the point of view of God. Through the Eucharist, God enters our world and we enter God's. The stories of Scripture, the prayers of the liturgy, and the actions of the community inform our imaginations to give us a vision of what life looks like under God's rule.

The Eucharist is to be a paradigm of a shared and sharing life. Participating in the Eucharist fosters participating in a communal life of interdependence marked by the virtue of solidarity among all. Solidarity is not a vague feeling of compassion at the misfortunes of others but rather a firm determination to commit ourselves to promoting the conditions necessary so that the good of all will flourish. Unfortunately, we often miss this connection. But separating liturgy from solidarity and its call to justice is not new. St. Paul criticized the church in Corinth for profaning the Lord's Supper by not attending to the needs of others (1 Cor 11:17-34). The prophets of old spoke out against religious ritual unrelated to moral commitment reminding Israel that worship is empty without social responsibility (Amos 5:21-24; Isa 1:10-17; Isa 58). The prophet Micah asks about the kind of liturgy God desires. The answer is a formula for a way of life: to do justice, to love kindness, and to walk humbly with God (Mic 6:8). The test of our worship is in the quality of our commitment to justice and not in what we get out of it for private benefit.

Participating in worship can and ought to foster a sense of solidarity with those with whom we worship and for whom we pray, even if we don't know them personally. Since solidarity is not limited to caring only for friends or family, the Eucharist can school us in solidarity by providing experiences where bonds of affection with others have a chance to grow. That is, the Eucharist can express praise and thanks to God while it also engages people in sharing. We see this happening as we engage the multicultural nature of the church by celebrating each other's special festivals (Guadalupe, St. Patrick's, or Tet, the Vietnamese New Year, for example). Suburban parishes can partner with the less-well-off urban or mission parishes to share resources. Ecumenical projects can bring various religious traditions together around a common cause. These are all ways to foster solidarity in a worshiping community so that the "Amen" we proclaim when receiving the Body of Christ in communion becomes a commitment to live in a life-giving way with the whole Body of Christ.

In short, worship not only shapes the way we see the world but also affects the way we are disposed to act in certain ways toward the world. To say that we love God in worship but that we are not disposed to the moral practice of loving and serving others is to misunderstand what makes for authentic worship. As we read in the First Letter of John, anyone who claims to love God but hates the neighbor is a liar (1 John 4:20-21). We cannot pretend to be relating to God whom we cannot see if we refuse to deal with our neighbors whom we can see. Worship schools the imagination and inclines our dispositions toward virtue.

Thus, the Eucharist as a spiritual practice is a focused opportunity to be addressed by God and a visible way to respond to God in the Spirit and to our belonging to one another in the Body of Christ. As it is with prayer and other spiritual practices, when we celebrate the Eucharist with the right intention, it has the power to transform our imagination and our moral sensibilities so that our experience of being loved can give rise to a virtuous life that will extend the range of love's influence in the world.

## Developing Virtue

Spirituality does not become authentic until it makes a difference in the way we live our lives. Remember, the measures of our spirituality are the fruits of the Spirit and the way we treat one another (see esp. Mark 12:29-31; Gal 5:22-23; and Matt 25). Whether spirituality makes a difference depends on whether we develop a way of being that is inspired by what lies deeply within us. Throughout the Christian tradition, this way of being inspired by the Spirit was expressed in terms of virtue.

For a long time now, we have grown accustomed to approaching the moral life as though it were filled with problems that needed to be solved. To determine right from wrong, we turned to principles or rules that would help us recognize our duty. Or, we looked to the consequences a possible action would produce. Or, we used a mix of principles and consequences to determine the right thing to do. As important as it is to decide the right action to take, we ought not to make the heart and soul of the moral life a matter of principles and consequences reigning over our thoughts and actions. There is another way to understand the moral life that goes back to the ancient Greeks and has remained with us in both the Christian spiritual and moral traditions. It is the way of virtue where our actions are determined by habits formed in light of a conception of the good life.

Instead of asking "What should I do?" the way of virtue asks questions just as important and that ought to be asked first: Who am I? What sort of person do I want to become? How am I going to get there?[18] This mode of ethics is more interested in our moral character than in a model of decision making. So rather than giving priority to principles and consequences, the way of virtue focuses on what it means to be a good person and to live a good life. Right and wrong are derived from that. The way of virtue brings together who we are and what we do. It serves a morally integrated spirituality for pastoral ministry well, for if there is any profession where the medium and the message are so closely tied together, it is the ministry. We judge the effectiveness of ministers not so much on their pastoral skills as on their integrity. Is what we do congruent with who we are?

The Greeks used the word "virtue" (*arête*) to express "excellence." They understood virtue in relation to the *telos*, the end or purpose of a being. Anything could have the quality of *arête*, or virtue, if it fulfills its end. A knife, for example, is excellent or has "virtue" when it cuts well, for that is the purpose of being a knife. When "virtue" is used of a person, it means that we are being good and living well. But the human *telos* is not a static state. It is a way of living that manifests virtues in the fullest or best possible way. Virtues and their corresponding activities both lead to and constitute the human *telos*. For Aristotle, the human *telos*, or best life for us to live, is to reason well and act accordingly. He called living this way "happiness." Aquinas fundamentally agrees with Aristotle that good character is necessary for humans to flourish and that living according to reason will lead to a good life. But Aquinas, along with the larger Christian tradition, also believed that we are made for a spiritual end—ultimate union or friendship with God. We fulfill this purpose by using our intellect to know God and our will to love God by cooperating with God's grace of infused virtues (faith, hope, and charity) and by acquiring the habits of the moral virtues.

Virtue, in its primary sense, reflects not the good that we do (the action) but the goodness of the actor (the morally good person). While we recognize virtue in behavior (and so talk of virtuous thoughts, feelings, or acts), virtues are rooted in the person as habits that help us to discern what to do so that we can live well and be good people. It makes no sense, then, to speak of "virtuous" thoughts or feelings that are unaccompanied by actions that lead to full human flourishing. To feel generous but not to follow through with a generous act is not enough to qualify as a "virtuous" person. We need virtues if we are to develop our full potential as human beings, for virtues lead to actions that express us at our best. Virtues are our way to goodness and holiness. They connect us to actions and ultimately to God.

For the purposes of shorthand, I like to think of virtues metaphorically as "habits of the heart" inclined toward values. "Of the heart" says that virtues are rooted someplace inside us and are ultimately a matter of love. Doing the right thing for the wrong reason is not a virtue and does not make the agent virtuous. "Habit" suggests not unthinking Pavlovian-like reaction, but acting by inclination and seemingly without effort. Acting by inclination is possible because virtue as "habit" connects head, heart, and hands. Unifying the whole self in a dynamic way makes acting from virtue neither mindlessly blind nor emotionally numb. Reason, will, emotions, and the body work together to respond appropriately to the situation. Once acquired, patterns of habituation intuitively incline us to know what to do and motivate us to act swiftly and reliably without having to stop and think about what to do every time we do it. The

Thomistic moral tradition speaks of this kind of moral awareness proper to virtue as "connatural knowledge," a rapid, penetrating, intuitive ability to know without thinking.[19]

Connatural knowledge reminds us that while we can reach a correct judgment by the right use of reason, there is another way. It is the way of the heart, the normal way a good person knows. When we are unable to rely on our ability to know connaturally, we turn to discursive reasoning from principles or consequences. Knowledge of the heart is attuned to the good because acquired virtue gives us a fine capacity for perception, or a felt resonance between our own being and the truth of the object of our attention. A skilled artist who can distinguish in an instant a fake from the real masterpiece demonstrates this way of knowing that comes with virtue.[20] Sometimes vocation directors and formation personnel demonstrate this capacity in judging the suitability of candidates. Their intuitive judgment is the result of years of experience in working with candidates and making connections between a candidate's character traits and the virtues necessary for a successful life in ministry.

The influence of one's character and virtue on the ability to size up the suitability of a person for a mission is well illustrated in the account of the polar explorer Ernest Shackleton. He interviewed over five thousand volunteers for the voyage of the *Endurance*, bound for Antarctica. In selecting his crew,

> Shackleton's method would appear to have been almost capricious. If he liked the look of a man, he was accepted. If he didn't, the matter was closed. And these decisions were made with lightening speed. There is no record of any interview that Shackleton conducted with a prospective expedition member lasting much more than five minutes. . . . Despite the instantaneous nature of these decisions, Shackleton's intuition for selecting compatible men rarely failed.[21]

The reliability of Shackleton's connatural intuitions was verified in that he lost no one throughout the two year ordeal of surviving shipwreck in Antarctica. This affective way of knowing that is characteristic of the virtuous is the normal way a good person knows what to do. The virtuous have a "nose" or a "taste" for the features of a situation that invite a response consistent with what virtue demands.

"Habit" also helps us understand virtue as an attribute acquired by practice. Aristotle saw that the way we develop in virtue is akin to becoming a great artist. We learn by practicing our craft: "People become builders by building and instrumentalists by playing instruments. Similarly we become just by performing just acts, temperate by performing temperate ones, brave by performing brave ones."[22] The ancients were impressed with the long years of sheer practice (habituation) necessary to become a thoroughly good person. We moderns might be just as impressed. In his book *Outliers*, Malcolm Gladwell uncovers the secret of people who are excellent at their craft. He says that these people spend ten thousand hours of practice before they hit their stride that puts them at the top of their game. "Practice," he says, "isn't the thing you do once you're good. It's the thing you do that makes you good."[23] Once acquired by practice, the virtues and their corresponding activities become second nature to us.

But the practice we do to acquire the virtue (our ten thousand hours) should not be confused with merely repeating behavior that externally conforms to that of a virtuous person. Mimicking behavior does not make us virtuous, though it may put us on the right path. We only become virtuous by doing virtuous deeds the way a virtuoso does them. Becoming virtuous is a process of formation that requires not only virtuous models to imitate but also instruction, encouragement, choice, and discipline. A habit moves toward a virtue when it is done attentively, with the right intention, and with the right feelings. Repeating the interior actions along with the external action puts us on the way to virtue.[24] Only gradually do we develop the internal dispositions that match our external behaviors.

For example, the predisposition to be grateful gets drawn out when our parents affirm us for saying "Thank you" and punish us when we don't. As children, being grateful is still largely a superego function. We repeat the external action of saying "thanks," but this is not yet expressing a virtuous disposition, even though our gratitude may appear to be virtuous. If we continue to repeat the behavior of saying "thanks," we may learn to appreciate the value of being grateful as part of what it means to live a good life, whether we get praised for it or not. So there is something to say for rote behavior in the process of becoming virtuous. Eventually, by repeating the intention to be grateful and by purposefully saying "Thank you" and being affirmed in doing so, we gradually become disposed to being grateful, whether our parents are watching us or not. We don't stop and ask, "What good is it to be grateful here?" We just do it. This is a sign that the habit of gratitude has taken on the form of a virtuous disposition and has become second nature to us. Aristotle would call this way of saying "Thanks" acting *from* virtue—that is, from the internalized disposition that is our character trait—in contrast to acting *according to* virtue, or some external standard that tells us what to do whether we feel like it or not.[25]

To remain virtuous, we must continue to practice, reflect on our practice, and strive to be our best. Virtues orient us toward excellence, toward being "all that we can be," to borrow the one-time Army recruiting slogan. For the virtuous, goodness is more than doing one's duty or following a rule. It is striving to be our best. Minimalism and mediocrity have no place among the virtuous. They are the first steps toward the deterioration of virtue. Not to exercise a virtue is to weaken it as a skill for being good. Daily practice matters. But we don't have to be perfect to be good. Growth and development are key features of virtue ethics. We are always on the way to becoming virtuous. Acquiring virtue requires the efforts of a lifetime. Remember Gladwell's ten thousand–hour rule!

Accordingly, whether we become virtuous or not is largely a matter of living from day to day doing things over and over with the intention to embody values that make us good, to think and to act in the way a virtuous person does, and to counteract contrary desires.

As with any habit, when we do something often enough we take on the quality of that action. Virtues depend on carving a pattern in the longings of the heart. Or, as brain scientists would have it, those ten thousand hours of practice carve a neurological pathway of myelinated sheaths from one neuron to another. Daniel Coyle's *The Talent Code* gives an account of neurological studies that show how the more a thought or action is done, the more the myelin is laid down over the pathway to make the neural connections fire more quickly and the behavior comes more easily.[26] Repetition is invaluable. As Coyle describes, if you want to get a skilled athlete or musician to flub up, don't let them practice.[27] Gradually the thoughts and actions that we repeat become part of who we are from doing them over and over. In matters of virtue, we become compassionate by intentionally making ourselves available to the needs of others and then purposefully responding to them in an appropriate way. We become generous by purposefully curbing our tendencies to selfishness and then offering ourselves in reasonable ways to others. Over time, acting compassionately or generously is delightful for us; it is our happiness, not an onerous duty. Eventually it feels utterly natural to act in these ways, as if we had possessed these virtues all along.

From the perspective of forming character through practice, every day matters. The moral life is going on continually. Everything we do has moral relevance to our character. There are no morally free zones when it comes to virtue. We draw on our character all the time, and not just for the occasional hard choice. In fact, the significant moral choices relative to character are not the ones we make in a crisis but in the small daily efforts that cultivate good habits of gratitude, generosity, compassion, courage, and the like. In matters of virtue, the ordinary is the realm of the moral. The real work of making big decisions happens in the quality of how we live our everyday lives leading up to the bigger decisions. If we want to be able to make a virtuous decision in the hard, ambiguous times, then we need to develop the habit of virtue in daily affairs. We are influencing the development or decay of our character all the time.

What we do influences who we become, and who we become in turn influences what we do. A moral feedback loop functions here. We acquire a virtuous character through the hard work of making the right choice over and over again. The habit of making the right choice makes it easier to choose well again because we have acquired the virtue that trains us to exercise our freedom rightly the next time we have a chance. As we deliberately choose the good, aware that we could choose otherwise, we grow in virtue. If we want to be a better person, then we need to recognize and to take the opportunities we have to do better. Just as one swallow does not make a summer, one random act of kindness does not make us virtuous. But it is a start. The practice of kindness will habituate us or form in us a settled disposition to act kindly. So, if we want to become more loving, peaceful, generous, sincere, and friendly, then we have to act in those ways when we have the chance. Our *telos* is always out ahead of us calling us forward to a fuller realization of being a good person and living a good life.

Christians know something of the *telos* of the good life because we have seen it in Jesus, our paradigmatic model of the virtuous life. We turn to Jesus to see who we are called to be. In him we find what constitutes good character, what counts as virtuous behavior, and what the good life looks like. While not setting out to repeat slavishly what Jesus did as though we were his mimics, we strive to make our lives a faithful variation of his own. In time we identify with the virtues that dispose us to live a life worthy of Christian discipleship, whether or not an obligation is prescribed by duties or principles and whether or not anyone is watching to supervise us. "One test of character and virtue," William F. May once said, "is what a person does when no one is watching."[28] Virtues link us to action by leaning us toward what living as a disciple demands.

The "habitual" nature of virtue gives stability to character and momentum to moral living that does not go into reverse easily. When we do something often enough, we take on the quality of that action. What we do in every moment and in each circumstance either contributes to the growth of virtue or not. Purposeful behavior has an effect not only on the world but also on the kind of person we are becoming. We become what we do. By habitually having the intention to tell the truth, for example, and expressing that intention in action, we gradually shape ourselves into truthful persons who can be trusted to be honest. Honesty is a virtuous disposition that we have nurtured through practice. Once acquired, the virtue gives us stability as a person characterized as being honest, and it gives us momentum to be honest in the future. So the kinds of habits we form prior to entering ministry, as well as those we acquire in ministry, influence a great deal the kind of ministers we become and the style our ministry will take.

But character, while stable, is not fixed in stone. Character traits get shaped and reshaped by our actions, by our experiences, and by our reflection on what they mean to us. We are all works in progress. No one is finished. Conversion is always possible. But the arc of changing character is long, not short. It doesn't come easily and without intention. We must be intentional about changing our habits if we want to refashion our character.

These then are four goals of the Christian spiritual journey. Becoming human makes the spiritual journey a communal adventure; imitating Christ keeps Jesus as the paradigm and norm of living faithfully in response to God; practicing the faith through devotional disciplines opens our hearts to the presence of God's Spirit and expresses our love for God; and developing virtue is our way of aspiring to holiness by becoming good. Each of these goals shows how the spiritual life is intimately involved with the moral life. Without spirituality, the moral life is rootless; but without morality, the spiritual life is fruitless. The next section explores the virtues that form the way to goodness and holiness for pastoral ministers.

# How Will
# We Get There?

# 2

# Developing Humanly

Amorally integrated spirituality for pastoral ministers requires sound human development for, as the theological axiom has it, "grace builds upon nature, but does not replace it." Ministry mediates God's love largely through the kind of person we are. Four virtues in the area of human development contribute to being a clear sign and agent of God's love—gratitude, humility, fidelity, and self-care.

### Gratitude

Gratitude is the foundational virtue for being human before God. Why? Because of grace. God speaks first in matters spiritual and moral, and the word God speaks is grace—unconditional love flowing throughout our lives, always and everywhere. When we begin with grace, we set the whole spiritual and moral life on the foundation of our belief in a beneficent God. That is, we believe that all that God has created is good and that God wills our well-being along with the well-being of the whole universe. God sees us as worthy of love and wants nothing more than to fill our lives with blessings.

With grace as the first word in the spiritual life, "thanks" is the second. Grace and gratitude go together like fire and heat, voice and sound, thunder and lightning. When we begin with a blessing that emphasizes God's unmerited favor on us, then we cannot help but respond with gratitude. It becomes the basic motive governing the whole of our lives. It's the first answer to the question, "Why be moral at all?" We want to be good and do what is right principally because we are grateful for grace—for the ways we have been loved by God.[1] Gratitude permeates what it means to be human in relation to God and to all that God has given us. Ingratitude, the failure to recognize grace and the tendency to take the bounty around us for granted or to feel entitled to it as a right, is an enormous spiritual failure and the root of sin.

No wonder St. Paul preaches gratitude as a spiritual imperative. He models grateful living in the way he begins nearly all his letters with a word of thanks, and he frequently exhorts his hearers to be grateful always and for everything (1 Thess 5:18; Phil 4:6-7; Col 3:15-17). From a Christian point of view, we cannot understand our relationship to God apart from first being receivers of God's gift of love. Gratitude is the response that affirms this bond between giver and receiver. It is the appropriate spiritual attitude and moral response to the experience of God's goodness. No wonder Ronald Rolheiser can make gratitude one of his nonnegotiable essentials of the spiritual life by saying, "To be a saint is to be fueled by gratitude, nothing more and nothing less."[2]

Nevertheless, despite such a strong theological grounding for making it the foundational attitude and governing worldview for the spiritual and moral life, gratitude still has a hard time getting a foothold so as to become second nature to us. Our social setting and cultural style resist it. We prize self-sufficiency. We want to get along by ourselves, be independent. But receiving a gift creates a bond of dependency with the giver that we find hard to accept. Moreover, we live at a time marked by advances in human rights and personal liberties. These displace gratitude with the more familiar attitude of entitlement—"I deserve it," we say. Such an attitude easily takes life for granted and fosters the expectation that we are owed something—whether that be as simple as someone cooking our meals and doing our laundry or as complex as providing unlimited health-care services. Even our prayer life can be consumed with asking for favors. And the more favors we get the more we crave. Our dissatisfaction with what we have is a bottomless pit. The desire for more is crystallized in the famous response of J. Paul Getty, the world's first billionaire, to the reporter's question, "When do you know that you have enough?" Mr. Getty thought a moment and said, "Not quite yet." When we always want more, we too easily become blind to what we have. If gratitude is to become our basic attitude toward life, then we need to think beyond the economics and politics that take life for granted and that believe more is always better.

That we all live with a governing perspective on life is inevitable. It is up to us to determine what the fundamental stance will be that shapes how we interpret what is going on and how we are to respond to it. For some, unfortunately, this stance is egocentric. These are often the ones who try to turn everything into possessions that never become gifts. Such a stance has no place among Christian ministers. When we begin with grace, we give "Thanks" for being surrounded by gifts that can never become possessions. For those whose inner eyes are opened to the amazing fact that grace is everywhere, everything coming to us is seen as gift to be shared. When grace has the first word, then the whole of our lives becomes an exchange of gifts. When we realize how much we have been given, we are moved to share it. We are indebted to one another and enjoy this mutual indebtedness by living with the dynamic of receiving and giving with grateful hearts. Notice how different it feels when we serve out of a spirit of gratitude for gifts received rather than out of guilt for what we owe. To say "thank you" to one another is to say "we belong together."[3]

The commission Jesus gave his apostles when he sent them on their first missionary journey can be loosely translated as "give freely to others what you have received freely as grace" (Matt 10:8). This biblical imperative identifies gratitude as the foundational virtue that seeks to imitate God's gracious action toward us. It is confirmed in the story of the healing of the ten lepers (Luke 17:11-19), the story used as the gospel text for Thanksgiving Day. The leper who returned to say "Thank you" had the special quality of recognizing grace—that undeserved blessing that lies behind everything in our lives. Recognizing grace focuses our attention on gratitude as the attitude that acknowledges that all that we have and are comes to us as gift. The dramatic event of the leper's healing opens the way to see that every event in our life is filled with grace. We can ask of even the most ordinary happenings, "How is God at work here?" Recognizing God's acting beneficently toward us moves us to act lovingly toward others. That is what gratitude does. It refuses to remain private. It reverberates throughout our relationships to make our interdependence a bond of give-and-take.

"Thank you." What could be simpler? We learned these words of appreciation very early on as a primary means of building social rapport. They have recently become the subject of psychological studies that show how gratitude serves as a reinforcer to encourage positive behavior, functions as a moral barometer of our affective response to being treated well, and motivates us to treat others as well as we have been treated.[4] Robert Emmons, in his popular book of positive psychology *Thanks!* studies gratitude as a crucial component of happiness. For him gratitude is the "knowing awareness that we are the recipients of goodness."[5]

Gratitude acknowledges goodness in our life and recognizes whence it comes. We nurture gratitude through memory. Remembering, in fact, is what gratitude likes to do best. For example, in the United States we have designated a day for the nation to remember the year's harvest. We call it Thanksgiving. We interrupt our normal pace of life to "go over the hills and through the woods" to gather and to give thanks with and for family, friends, and food.

As religious believers, we remember, above all, that God is the giver of gifts. John Shea tells the story of one young boy finding God this way. We pick up on the story when the family shares a group grace before a festive meal. It is the five-year-old boy's turn to pray:

He began by thanking the turkey which, although he had not yet tasted it, he was sure would be good. This was a novel piece of gratitude and he followed it with more predictable credits given to his mother for cooking the turkey and his father for buying it. Then he began a chain of thank-yous, surfacing hidden benefactors and linking them together. "And the checker at the Jewel, and all the Jewel people, and the farmers who feed the turkeys to get them fat, and the people who make the feed, and the people who bring the turkeys to the store . . ." His little Colombo mind was playing detective, tracing the path of the turkey to his plate. This litany went on for some time and ended with, "Did I forget anyone?"

"God," said his older brother.
"I was just getting to him," the child solemnly said, unflustered.[6]

To remember in thanksgiving is also to remember times when we thought we would not make it—someone died whom we loved and needed; we lost a job; we got divorced; we were terribly sick. We remember that we were ready to give up. But we didn't. We remember that we are here. We made it! We got through the worst day of our life. When we see where we are, making our way out of the dark, we remember that we could not have made it to today if we had only ourselves to depend on. We remember that a strength other than our own pulled us through, a wisdom greater than our own opened the way. When we look back over what we have received and see where others have extended themselves to us, we are seeing the work of God's grace. Remembering is the way of letting the love of God touch us again as we relive those graced moments of our lives.

Gratitude also affirms our fundamental religious conviction that we are not our own explanation for living. We owe all we have and are to something beyond ourselves. That is why we can chuckle at Bart Simpson when he gathers his family for dinner and prays, "Dear God, we paid for all this stuff ourselves, so thanks for nothing." We chuckle because we see the bigger picture that he misses. We know that we are more receivers than achievers. While the Simpsons may very well have earned their money, they are missing the goodness that comes independently of their efforts, including the opportunity given to earn the money in the first place. When we remember, we know whom to thank, and we see that we are here today because of grace.

The Eucharist is our chief spiritual practice of remembering grace. No wonder we make it one of our central spiritual practices. At the Last Supper, Jesus instructed his followers to "do this in remembrance of me" (Luke 22:19); and, as the preface of the eucharistic prayer reminds us, we are "always and everywhere to give thanks." In the Eucharist, we gather to thank God for being the recipients of gifts freely bestowed. But eucharistic spirituality does not leave us complacent with the satisfaction that we live by grace. Rather, eucharistic remembering nurtures these gifts and directs us to give freely what we have been freely given. We celebrate the Eucharist as a judgment against ourselves if we fail to develop our gifts and hoard what we have received as a possession to be protected and not as a gift to be shared.

Gratitude as a virtue is a disciplined way of living. Like all virtues, it comes by choice and through practice. Each time we choose to be grateful, the next choice is a little easier, a little less self-conscious. But still the choice to be grateful does not come without effort. As James Gustafson is quick to remind us, the affirmation on which gratitude depends—that God is good and wills our well-being—is only in part confirmed by experience.[7] In the face of the misfortunes of so many, belief in God's beneficence is hard to hang onto. It is difficult to be grateful to God, for example, when those whom we have trusted betray us, or when the church gets racked with scandal and we are forever looked upon with suspicion. It is difficult to be grateful when innocent children are painfully and brutally taken from us through random acts of violence in a schoolyard, or when all that we worked for in building a home or small business is swept away by a financial crisis, a hurricane, flood, or fire. We must be careful not to push past hard experiences like these to an easy *Deo gratias* (Thanks be to God) when life is tough.

Gratitude does not take away the horror of evil. That is why I am always moved by the survivors who can still find reason to be grateful in the face of atrocities that would seem to make grousing trump gratitude. Yet they do not point to those who are better off, or pity themselves for having gotten the worst of it, or look for what is missing in their lives, or rehearse the "if onlys" that would have made everything turn out differently. They can wrap themselves in resentment if they want. They have every reason to do so, and no one would fault them if they did. But they seem to choose not to. When collapsing into the arms of despair would be perfectly understandable, they lean into their belief in God's goodness and care. They look over life with the attitude that God is in charge, and they find reason to thank God for the good experiences of the past, though these may have come with less frequency than desired. They embody St. Paul's conviction that "all things work together for good for those who love God" (Rom 8:28). The goodness that they know, even in the worst of times and in smaller sizes than they would like, is there as a gift of God and of caring friends. About the presence of thankfulness in the face of unmerited evil, Robert Emmons concludes that "gratitude is not simply a form of 'positive thinking' or a technique of 'happyology,' but rather a deep and abiding recognition and acknowledgment that goodness exists under even the worst that life offers."[8]

In short, grateful people are, at the bottom, happy with themselves, with others, and with what they have. Even under adverse conditions, grateful people are not miserable. Because of gratitude they choose not to let destruction and death have dominion over them. They live with the abiding confidence that God is love, that goodness exists, that the universe is ultimately a friendly place.

Some practices that cultivate and express gratitude are:[9]

- taking an inventory of the ways we have been gifted by others;
- naming the people in our life who have made a difference for us;
- practicing the presence of God;
- celebrating the Eucharist with memories of being graced;

- developing our own gifts and nurturing the gifts of others;
- writing a "Thank you" note for a gift received;
- giving a gift as a sign of appreciation.

## Humility

The humble witness to gratitude, for they know that we are more gift than achievement. Humility is the virtue that recognizes that we are all the beneficiaries of the gifts of others. Humility calls us to share ourselves as gift for the sake of the well-being of others without the expectation that someone will notice it.

Humility is not only a tough virtue to understand but an even harder one to acquire. For one thing, we easily get so wrapped up in ourselves that we overestimate our abilities and way of seeing the world. Since we are predisposed to think our vision is clear and our way is the right way, we do not readily see things as they are. But humility respects the way things are in its commitment to stand with what is so. A scene from John Steinbeck's *East of Eden* says it well. Samuel Hamilton is a model of humility, someone everyone recognizes as having sterling character. Lee, his Chinese servant, speaks pidgin English because he knows that no one would listen to him if he didn't. People just expect him to speak that way. With Samuel, however, he speaks perfectly correct English. He explains himself to Samuel, "You are one of the rare people who can separate your observation from your preconception. You see what is, where most people see what they expect."[10] Lee is right. Samuel is rare. Most of us see what we expect to see, not what is. The myopia of our own narcissism distorts our world. We engage the world in terms of its ability to satisfy us. But humility requires that we see clearly what is.

To acquire the virtue of humility, we need good models, like Samuel Hamilton, to imitate. But one thing Samuel would never do is tell us how humble he is. Who would ever believe or be drawn to someone who wore humility on their sleeve? The humble are unobtrusive. Humility is a quiet virtue.[11] Humility that is conscious of how it appears is not true humility. The humble allow their actions to speak for them without needing to draw attention to themselves. A quote from an author unknown (how appropriate) summarizes it well: "There is no limit to what can be done if it doesn't matter who gets the credit."[12]

That the community of the faithful across denominational lines is looking for such a character trait in their ministers was confirmed by the *Profiles in Ministry* project of the Association of Theological Schools in the United States and Canada. This project revealed that one of the traits most desired in a minister was to be able to provide service without regard for public recognition.[13] The faithful are looking for ministers who are humble.

Humility brings the freedom of not having to make oneself the center of attention. When we are free from worrying about how we will come across, then we are free for focusing better on what needs to be done. This is the humility of God shown in the incarnation and on the cross. St. Paul gives us the template for humility in his exhortation to the Philippians: "Do nothing from selfish ambition or conceit, but in humility regard others as better than yourselves. Let each of you look not to your own interests, but to the interests of others" (Phil 2:3-4). St. Paul follows this immediately with the great hymn of the self-emptying love of Christ that expresses the attitude that we are to have in the imitation of Christ (Phil 2:6-11).

In short, the humble are not preoccupied with themselves but with the service they are providing. They do not need to proclaim their altruistic greatness or fill their speech with self-references by saying, "Hey, look at me. Pay attention! Notice what I did." They remain incognito. The healthily humble do not spend time keeping up appearances or projecting an image to impress others with qualities they don't have. The humble are more concerned that good be done than they are that others think well of them or recognize them for what they do.

Another reason that humility is hard to develop is that we often miss the truly humble because we confuse them with fraudulent forms of humility, such as thinking less of one's self than others do, or discounting one's gifts, or being overly submissive, or displaying uncritical docility that is unwilling to take a risk by offering one's own opinion. The humility that uses insincere flattery to suggest one's own inferiority is really arrogance in disguise. It puffs up the other so as to position the self to take advantage of the other's insecurity.

To understand humility properly as a virtue for ministry, it helps to remember that "humility" and "human" have the same word root: *humus* (earth). God took the dust of the earth, breathed into it, and brought forth the "earth creature" (Gen 2:7). We have been destined for humility ever since, and we are reminded of it in our Ash Wednesday liturgy, "Remember, you are dust and unto dust you shall return."

Humility, simply put, is being down-to-earth about oneself. It is the practical effect of accepting oneself as creature and not the Creator. Humility does not deny having gifts, but it submits to the truth of the limits of our power, of what we can do and of what we cannot do. The great challenge for being humble is to be true to our creaturely condition. As creatures of God, we have dignity not deity, yet the temptation is to distort our place in the world and want to play God. Humility emerges from the realistic acceptance of who we are. Joseph Gallagher, a former professor of mine, gave us the best functional definition of humility I have ever heard. "Humility," he said, "is the willingness to be what you are and to do what you can." This clearly situates humility between the extremes of pride (acting as though we had no limits) and self-effacement (ignoring our real abilities and accomplishments).

Humility is the willingness to be what we are. The first movement toward humility is to cultivate our capacity for true self-knowledge about what we can and cannot do in the world.[14] True humility remains elusive, however, in a society where so many do not have an adequate sense of self or self-worth. Granted, the question "Who am I?" takes a lifetime to answer. Yet we put ourselves well on the road when we make good use of whatever means are available to facilitate the critical self-reflection that helps us understand who we are. These means can be anything from professional psychological services of therapy, psychometric inventories, or dreamwork, to the habit of a prayerful examination of conscience and regular reflection on life experiences with the aid of a journal, spiritual companion, or good friends. Until we gain some grasp of who we are and some basic level of self-esteem, there is little likelihood for acquiring healthy humility.[15]

Critical self-knowledge begins with recognizing and accepting that we are creatures, not the Creator. This means that we are gifted to do some things, but we do not have all the gifts to do everything. We are limited and dependent. But we bridle at limits and dependence. We want to make it on our own, be self-reliant. But we can't. The humble stand in contrast to the arrogance like that of the Babylonians who, in the words of Isaiah, proclaimed, "I am, and there is no one besides me" (Isa 47:10). Such a delusional belief that we need only ourselves and need not be responsible to or for anyone else is the height of narcissistic arrogance.[16] Reality for the humble, by contrast, is dependence—ultimately utter dependence on God. We are not separate individuals who can each follow our own desires. We are linked with each other, united with Christ in one body. Learning dependence on God and interdependence with all of God's creation is the road to healthy humility.

Humility grows in proportion to our capacity to see ourselves interdependently. For example, our very physical being depended on others to come to be. That we continue to survive depends on the care and know-how of others. We eat what others have sown, harvested, and prepared. We speak a language others have coined. We enjoy rights for which others have died. To be so dependent is not to be humiliated but to be invited to share these gifts with others who also depend on us. We cannot be humble as long as we persist in the belief that we can stand on our own. Humility grows out of being aware of our dependence on one another and on God. When we fail to accept the limitations and dependence of our creatureliness, we fail to grasp the very roots of humility.

My favorite lesson on facing limits humbly comes from Ernest Hemingway's *The Old Man and the Sea*. In this story, Santiago, a Cuban fisherman, hooks a fish of heroic proportions. He lets out his line and follows the fish out to sea beyond the limits of its strength and his. Finally, on the way back to shore, sharks lock in on the fish lashed to the side of the boat. They attack and tear the great fish to pieces, despite the old man's valiant defense with knife, tiller, and oars. When only the eighteen foot skeleton of the fish remained, the old man confesses that he should not have gone out so far. Going beyond his limits ruined them both.[17]

As with the old man, so it is with us. Humility does not come easily. Like the old man, we too seem to have a particularly difficult time knowing our limits, knowing how much is enough and sticking with it. More often than is good for us, we go out too far. Theologically speaking, we would say that we run ahead of our graces. In pastoral ministry, this can take the shape of counseling cases beyond our competence or proposing parish projects that are beyond our resources of time, money, and personnel.

Our culture doesn't make it easy to be humble in this way. Our culture holds up an ideal self whose dignity depends on the ability to control outcomes. And if there is one criticism of people in ministry that I hear often it is that we love to be in control. But humility forces us to ask to what extent is living with absolute control the only kind of life worth living? Certainly no one wants to deny that we need some degree of freedom and control if we are to respect personal dignity. But the freedom of humility is less the freedom to control outcomes and more the freedom to choose an attitude. Recall what Viktor Frankl said in his reflection on surviving the concentration camps: "The last of the human freedoms [is] to choose one's attitude in any given set of circumstances, to choose one's own way."[18] This is the freedom born of the virtue of humility.

Humility checks our passion for control by enabling us to take a lighter grasp on life, to live with limits, to choose to play the hand we have been dealt, and to let go of what cannot be ours. It is able to pray with confidence Psalm 131, a prayer of humble trust: "O LORD, my heart is not lifted up, my eyes are not raised too high; I do not occupy myself with things too great and too marvelous for me. But I have calmed and quieted my soul like a weaned child with its mother; my soul is like the weaned child that is with me" (Ps 131:1-2).

Moreover, humility does not regard dependence an indignity. Accepting dependence can be a growing process, not a wilting one. Jesus showed in his suffering the dignity of dependence. In Gethsemane, we hear him plead with his disciples, "I am deeply grieved, even to death; remain here, and stay awake with me" (Matt 26:38). This dependence on others is a sign of a more radical dependence on God, for Jesus then threw himself on the ground and prayed, "My father, if it is possible, let this cup pass from me; yet not what I want but what you want" (Matt 26:39). Jesus shows that dependence is a call to be open to God, to see more clearly the limits of control. Humility recognizes that leaning on the strength of others and being open to their care is a necessary grace for living.

The fact that we are limited and dependent is clear. The question for humility as a virtue is, is that okay with us? Do we resent having to ask for help? Are we open to what we don't know or can't do? Do we lose our dignity and worth if we don't have absolute control, or can't do everything, or can't do perfectly even what we can do? Humble pastoral ministers know how to accept help without being humiliated. They can say "No" to requests that are beyond their limits without feeling guilty, and they can say "Thanks" to a compliment without having to make excuses. The humble are able to consent to, affirm, celebrate, and share who they are.

Humility is also the willingness to do what we can. That is to say, the humble are able to be part of the action, but they don't have to be the whole show. They can let go of what is beyond their ability and beyond their control and invite others in to share the burden and the benefit. The humble know that there is no life apart from the mutual participation in the life of each other, and they do what they can to honor and promote the relationships they live by. The growth of collegial collaboration among ministers is a sign of humility. The humble are able to contribute what they can, then stand back and trust in the gracious work of God acting through the gifts of others who can do what they cannot.

Signs of running ahead of our graces and assuming more control than is rightfully ours are behaviors such as growing cynical, anxious, depressed, or highly critical of others; losing faith in other people; becoming defensive, short-tempered, and suspicious of the basic honesty and goodwill of others. When we start to show signs like these, we need to ask just how much of the situation bothers us for objective reasons and how much bothers us because it reminds us of our own limitations that we do not want to accept. Without humility we tend to exaggerate our importance and put down others so that we feel more valuable. People who can't live with themselves as they are seem to try to do their best to make sure others can't either. Humility keeps us honest with what is troubling us so that we can deal with it as it is and not look for a scapegoat in other issues or other people.

The deadly enemy of humility is pride, the vice of self-inflation—thinking and acting as if we had no limits. Whereas humility lives with limits creatively and graciously, pride is grossly competitive. It is unable to enjoy an achievement for its own sake but only to the extent that it is better than someone else's. With a disposition like that, the proud make their gifts into walls that alienate rather than bridges that unite. Humility, on the other hand, enables us to affirm and to celebrate what we have, to recognize that even if we don't have it all we are still secure enough and good enough, and then to be open to what others can give.

Some practices that cultivate and express humility are:

- admitting that we don't have the answer when we really don't;
- working within the limits of our competence and asking for help when we need it;
- accepting a compliment without making excuses;

- acknowledging the accomplishments of another;
- saying "No" when our plate is full and we have no more time or energy;
- making an effort to perceive the other on the other's terms.

## Fidelity

To be in relationship is the basic law of human nature. We cannot understand what it means to be human apart from our relationship to God or from our relationships with one another and all of creation. Relationships are part of what makes us who we are. Goodness and holiness are, at bottom, about the quality of our relationships. Under "Becoming Human" as a goal of the spiritual life in the first chapter, I cited James Keenan's correlation of justice, fidelity, and self-care with our threefold relationships—to others in general, to specific others, and to self. I want to emphasize fidelity and self-care as part of the human dimension of ministry. I will consider justice under the pastoral dimension so as to underscore how pastoral ministry is enmeshed in a web of interrelationships.

Fidelity, and its synonyms of faithfulness, loyalty, reliability, constancy, and trustworthiness, is the virtue that nurtures the affective bonds that weave the fabric of our relationships. In the Old Testament, God's covenant contains the promise of abiding faithfulness. Covenantal love (*hesed*) is a promise of unconditional love and ongoing presence. Absolute fidelity is the substance of the first commandment of the Mosaic covenant. When Israel begins to blow kisses at calves and to worship foreign idols, the prophets call her back to covenantal loyalty. Even in the face of infidelity, the prophets declare God's fidelity (cf. Hos 11). In the New Testament, God's promise of steadfast loyalty is in Jesus. The very title, Christ, witnesses to Jesus' being the promised one of God, the Messiah, who fulfills the hopes of the covenant's promise of fidelity.

My favorite biblical stories that teach us about fidelity are the contrasting garden stories of Eden (Gen 2–3) and Gethsemane

(Matt 26), especially as retold by John Shea.[19] We pick up on the story of the Garden of Eden on the sixth day of creation when God entrusted the earth to the care of Adam and Eve and them to each other. The story is suffused with the sense that humanity is empowered with the capacity to influence creation and one another by being entrusted with gifts, the gifts of creation and the gifts of one another.

Into this ideal setting, the serpent enters to sow seeds of distrust. The serpent suggests to Adam and Eve that God cannot be trusted and so tempts them with power—the knowledge of good and evil. Adam and Eve choose to believe the snake and so miss the mark of remaining loyal to their commitment to God. They refuse to believe that God can be trusted, and they refuse to trust each other also. Their fall admits into the world alienation, betrayal, and the need to build protective defenses that keep others out and that keep the self secure. By distrusting God, Adam and Eve upset the way relationships ought to be. Separation, fear, and suspicion mark their lives. This is symbolized by their hiding in the bushes to protect themselves from God and by their sewing fig leaves for clothes to protect themselves from one another. Adam and Eve could no longer allow themselves to be vulnerable to God or to each other. The freedom that would have been theirs in a trusting relationship is lost, distorting the demands of sexuality, friendship, and social responsibility. The fear of distrust contaminates all relationships with suspicion.

The story of Gethsemane, on the other hand, is the story of Jesus trusting in God by not abandoning his mission. This garden story brings us back from the fear that tells us not to trust, not to trust God, not to trust anyone. Whereas Adam and Eve misused their freedom and became strangers, Jesus used his to make friends. In fact, some of his gatherings at dinner parties were so notorious for their mix of dinner guests that he shocked teachers of the law with a new image of who's in and who's out. Jesus lived for the sake of making everyone a friend of God and friends with one another.

Judas appears as the betrayer to highlight the centrality of fidelity as the disciple's character trait then and now. To violate fidelity through betrayal is not only to do the wrong thing but also to become the wrong kind of person. By violating fidelity, we are becoming a betrayer like Judas, failing to follow Jesus in imitating God's fidelity. Jesus' great act of covenantal fidelity was to accept death on the cross, trusting that his life would not evaporate into an empty future. Jesus lived trusting that he would be sustained by the undefeatable love of God. The resurrection was his vindication for being so trusting.

The stories of the two gardens teach us that we are sustained by the faithfulness of God. As emissaries of God, we are likewise called to imitate God by rooting our relationships in the virtue of fidelity. We are free to trust others because we know that we are trusted by God and trust in God. If we can let go of fear and suspicion so that we can see the other more as gift than as threat, then we will be able to answer what is of God in the other. This is a basic energy for ministry. To draw on it, we must redirect any preliminary hesitation away from suspicion and toward trust. What God has trusted, we must start trusting, whether that be our own goodness or the goodness of others. What God has been willing to take a risk on, we must be willing to take a risk on. Only when we start to trust ourselves will we be able to take full responsibility for the ministry to which we are called.

Nurturing fidelity in the world we know is not for the faint of heart. Our culture discourages fidelity in the way it prizes autonomy (why make any promises that will bind you to another?), celebrates novelty (why stick with anything for too long if it ties you down to the past?), and loves the disposable (why hang on to what no longer satisfies?). Then there is the pervasive competitive spirit in sports, politics, and the marketplace that conditions us to capitalize on our opponents' weaknesses, to be suspicious of any offer to cooperate, and to circle the wagons in defense of peers to protect them from attack and to save the public image of the company. It is no accident that this type of loyalty has spawned "spin doctors" to protect the powerful. Whistle-blowers have always suffered the fate of prophets from their own country for putting integrity and accountability above loyalty to the group when they expose crooks in the board-room, pedophiles in the clergy, dopers in the batter's box, or addicts and spousal abusers in the family. To balance loyalty and truth calls for keen discernment and great courage, two other virtues that intersect with fidelity.[20]

Nurturing fidelity in a disposable and competitive culture does not mean calling for misplaced surrender, or for the naïve gullibility that falls prey to the hucksterism of P.T. Barnum: "There is a sucker born every minute and two to take him." Fidelity is the virtue that counteracts the forces favoring fleeting commitments so that they do not dictate the terms of our relationships. It knows that our ex-periences are filled with ambiguity and our relationships are marked by a mix of motives. But fidelity refuses to become so suspicious as to be blind to anyone worthy of trust.

Those most worthy of trust are our friends. Friendship is both the school of fidelity and the arena in which to practice it. The spiri-tual life of ministers would shrivel without friends and their moral life would be crippled. After all, Genesis tells us, in the beginning, God saw that it was not good for us to be alone (Gen 2:18). Aristo-tle's great discourse on friendship teaches that living well includes functioning well as a social, relational being who shares life together with friends through thoughtful conversation, an exchange of ideas, and the cultivation of virtues that make life worth living.[21] To survive spiritually we need companions and the intimacy that friendship can bring, and to live morally we need the company of friends.

Friends shape us, inevitably. How different would our life be if certain people had not come to us when they did and the way they did? But these friends in ministry must be more than superficial acquaintances or codependent relationships. Paul Wadell's reflec-tion on friendship underscores how much friendship must be marked by mutuality and care for one another and for what we care about, by a desire for what is best for one another, by the commit-ment to seek one another's well-being, and by the freedom that allows for growth at each one's own pace. For Wadell, the connection between friendship and fidelity is inescapable because when other people enter our life who care about what we care about, they support us by caring about it with us.[22]

One of the best portrayals of what friendship is and can do is in the movie *Shadowlands*, the story of the marriage of C. S. "Jack" Lewis to Joy Gresham. When Jack first meets Joy, he is living the safe, predictable, and comfortable life of an Oxford don. They were married for only a few years when Joy fell ill with cancer and died. But during their brief time together, they were not only husband and wife but also best friends. They shared big things in common, like a vision of life, and they enjoyed the little things of everyday life, like conversation and time together. As best friends do, they drew out the best in each other and made each other better by helping each other grow in love and fidelity.[23] *Shadowlands* illustrates how fidelity between friends calls forth from each the rich potential that lies within both.

We can see ourselves in this story even if we are not married or in a committed partnership. We see ourselves because we know people who have entered our lives and have helped us become better than we could ever become by ourselves. It is no wonder that Aristotle said, "Without friendship no one would choose to live, even if they had all other good things in life."[24] An Aristotelian truism of living a fulfilled life is that we become good by spending time with good people. Through friends, we learn how to be faithful. Every friendship is a lesson in the discipline of fidelity because the nature of friendship is to teach us what fidelity demands. By being friends with a few we learn how to be friendly, and thus faithful, to many.

But a word of warning is now in order about friendships in pastoral ministry. In the practice of ministry we must be careful not to confuse the deeply personal and intimate relationship of friendship with our professional pastoral relationships. One of the easiest ways to misuse our pastoral role and fall into unprofessional conduct is to treat a professional pastoral relationship (those in which we are serving a religious need) just like a special friendship. They are not the same and need to be handled differently.

Whereas friendships are marked by mutuality and equality, professional relationships are unequal and one-directional. In a professional pastoral relationship, those to whom we minister place into our hands something of value to themselves. They entrust to us their secrets, sins, fears, hopes, and need for salvation. This act of entrusting creates a "fiduciary relationship." That is, in making this act of trust, they give us power over them and trust that we will not betray them by misusing that power. They trust we will not control, dominate, or manipulate them to serve our own interests in power, prestige, or pleasure. The vulnerability of a fiduciary relationship can stir up strong emotions and sexual desires in both partners. Keeping appropriate boundaries will not stifle these feelings, but boundaries do help us avoid acting on them. Since the pastoral minister is the one with the greater power in the relationship, it falls on the minister to guide the process of the relationship by safeguarding the vulnerability of those seeking pastoral service by holding in trust what they entrust to us. Fidelity to trust is the central obligation of and indispensable virtue in the pastoral relationship.

If we want to be virtuous in the way fidelity requires of the pastoral minister, then we need to engage in practices that strengthen fidelity: respect physical and emotional boundaries in a relationship; keep secret what has been confided to us; honor others even in their absence; don't become a source of gossip; protect another's best interest when in a position to do so. Moreover, one of the signs of growing in the virtue of fidelity is the ability to distinguish the various kinds of relationships we have with people. We have personal relationships with friends and neighbors, and professional relationships with business partners, employees, parishioners, students, and patients, for example. After recognizing these different kinds of relationships, we then need to manage each appropriately without confusing one with the other. We ought not to mix or confuse the equality and mutuality of personal relationships with professional pastoral relationships, such as when the pastor becomes the spiritual director of the secretary, or the youth minister dates someone from the youth group. These "dual relationships" threaten fidelity by harboring potential conflicts of interest that can lead to playing favorites or exploiting the other's dependency. One of the ways of managing our relationships well so that fidelity governs them is to practice good self-care. It is to the virtue of self-care that I will turn next.

Some practices that nurture and express fidelity are:

- avoiding unnecessary dual relationships and monitoring the inevitable ones;
- respecting the physical and emotional boundaries in a relationship;
- sharing dinner with friends and lingering longer over conversation;
- keeping secrets and not becoming a gossiper;
- sending a card or e-mail to keep in touch;
- showing up when we say we will show up.

## Self-Care

The spiritual life does not merely believe something about God, it also knows something about ourselves. The virtue of self-care is rooted in knowing that we are loved and have worth independently of our achievements. Self-care is about being responsible for ourselves through appropriate self-love. It is the foundation of everything we do—from the physical basics of preserving our health by eating properly, exercising, and getting sufficient sleep to the moral and spiritual basics of fostering our own identity and protecting our integrity by living true to our conscience. It is a virtue that is very much interrelated with the others and undergirds them. For example, without self-esteem, what looks like gratitude is really manipulation; humility is a silent scream for recognition; and fidelity is codependence. We can speak truth to power with courage when we accept our own worth; and we can give generously when we know that we don't have to buy our love because we are already loved without conditions.

Self-care as a virtue does not find an easy foothold in a culture that has often been characterized as self-centered. Nor does it fit easily into a tradition that has preached the importance of self-sacrifice and self-denial. But the second half of the Great Commandment tells us that self-love is important, for we are to love God and our neighbor *as we love ourselves* (Luke 10:27). Being good to ourselves makes it possible to be good to others.

My contention is that appropriate self-care is not selfishness and that authentic self-donation can only come from a place of strength we have by respecting ourselves and by being fully alive in the Spirit. Only those with a strong sense of their own worth can risk sacrifice, and only those who are first full of life can empty themselves. One of the great dangers along the spiritual journey is to exhort those who are still weak in their self-esteem or drained of life-giving energy to be self-sacrificing and self-denying. This can cause great harm spiritually and psychologically. The danger of selfishness masquerading as self-care always lingers. But the two need not be equated. Selfishness sees everything predominantly in relation to its own satisfaction: "It's all about me!" Self-care does not make our own good the measure of all value or give preference to self-interest at those times when we should yield to the needs of another.[25]

The theological grounding for self-care as a virtue goes back to the very grounds I established above for gratitude—God loves us. Remember, grace is the bedrock upon which we can build a life of virtue. The doctrines of creation, redemption, and sanctification are the theological housing for appropriate self-care. The first step in the spiritual and moral life is not what we do but rather what God first does on our behalf. God loves us and remains involved with us through acts of ongoing creation, through the life-death-resurrection of Jesus, and through the gift of the Spirit. Respecting our createdness through appropriate self-care is a form of grateful worship of God, giving thanks for being a reflection of divinity itself.

The incarnational principle (that God has become human) tells us that God loves us through us. Taking care of ourselves is our way of accepting God's love. Not to care for ourselves is to turn our back on cooperating with the love God has for us. This is sin, simply put. But cooperating with God's love calls us to a robust participation in our own lives by affirming and encouraging ourselves to enjoy what we are doing and to assume responsibility for who we are and who we can become by taking care of ourselves and developing our gifts.

Self-care begins with accepting God's love as the ground of our worth. Here is one of my favorite stories of accepting God's love:

> One evening as the priest walked along the country road he came across an old man also out enjoying the twilight air. They walked and talked together until a sudden rain made them take shelter. When their conversation moved into silence, the old Irishman took his little prayer book and began praying half aloud. The priest watched him a long while, then in a quiet whisper said, "You must be very close to God!" The old man smiled very deeply and answered, "Yes! He is very fond of me!"[26]

Each of us needs to be able to say with this old man, "God is very fond of me!" That may be our most difficult act of faith. But it is foundational to self-esteem, the most elementary aspect of appropriate self-care. The faith conviction that God loves us, that we are made in God's likeness, and that our basic identity and worth come from being a creation of God and not from our own achievement or anything else is a profound spiritual claim on which to build appropriate self-care.[27]

Self-esteem takes root in being blessed by others. "Do you love me?" is the persistent cry of the heart. We ask it of people significant to us and we ask it of God. We feel valuable when we know someone loves us. Our worth is first given to us, and then we claim it. To acquire self-esteem, we need to hear someone say to us, "I love you," and then we must believe it to be true.

The secret of Jesus' being able to live a life of freedom and fidelity in self-giving love was, I believe, his "Abba" experience of divine love. He accepted himself as being accepted by God. The gospel accounts of his baptism in the Jordan convey how Jesus must have experienced himself as someone special in God's eyes when he heard the blessing coming from the rip in the heavens: "This is my Son, the Beloved, with whom I am well pleased" (Matt 3:17; Mark 1:11; Luke 3:22). The rest of the gospel demonstrates the practical effect of living under the gaze of the Father's love and holding fast to these words of worth. Throughout his ministry, Jesus could look on the poor and hungry, the meek and marginalized and see them as blessed because he knew that God was seeing him and the world that way. Because he felt secure in the Father's love, Jesus knew whose he was and thus who he was. He did not have to latch on to his works of wonder to secure his identity or worth. He had it in being loved by God.

We feel valuable when we know that someone loves us. Unfortunately, too many of us do not live like Jesus. We live unsure that we are loved. We feel insecure and burdened by an abiding sense of unworthiness. Many factors can contribute to making low self-esteem the rule rather than the exception in our lives. What becomes our self-esteem is largely the product of how others relate to us, how they name us, what they tell us we are, the image we have of ourselves as a result, and how we value ourselves in that image. For example, to be told "You are the sunshine of my life" has a much different impact on our self-image than being put down with "You are such a jerk."

We pick up messages about ourselves primarily through relationships, especially our most influential ones with our parents, siblings, and teachers. We have all heard stories of how people were not always the object of unconditional acceptance—parents did not give their children the encouragement and affirmation they needed, siblings rejected them, and teachers mistreated them. In various degrees, all of us have picked up the brokenness these significant others projected onto us. We may still be carrying these negative messages around and letting them control how we feel about ourselves. Because of our familiarity with such cases, it is easy to understand Vivian's feelings in the movie *Pretty Woman*. After telling of how her mother mistreated her as a child by locking her in the attic as a punishment, Vivian says, "When people put you down enough, you start to believe it. The bad stuff is easier to believe." In addition to failures within our family system, low self-esteem may also result from being subjected to social prejudice and oppression. We see this when male-dominated structures do not honor women's gifts in society or the church, or when Caucasian-dominated structures oppress people of color.

Our images of God also have an influence on self-esteem as well as religious preaching and teaching. Most of us have picked up our images of God from the way we have been taught about God, especially through the way we have been treated in God's name. Images of God have a way of embedding themselves in elusive corners of our subconscious and we continue to burn incense at their shrines. Before we can experience the God who spoke words of worth to Jesus in the Jordan, we need to destroy a whole pantheon of false gods and distorted images, especially images of the "gotcha" god of moral perfectionism who keeps book on us and waits for us to trip up so that we can be marked a loser. If we believe God is like that, then surely we will have a hard time maintaining positive self-esteem.

Self-esteem shows up in our conduct, for we tend to relate to others in ways that reflect our own formation and the way we relate to ourselves. Anger, resentment, jealousy, revenge, and rivalry take over when we forget that God's love grounds us. Not sure that we are loved and loveable, we try to secure our worth in surrogate loves, like our achievements, our charm, our wit, or our bright ideas. But displacing divine love with these surrogate loves is nothing less than idolatry. As long as we confuse our worth with those self-created idols, we get trapped in self-absorbing fears and raise our defenses. We attack, put down, control, or dominate others in order to assure ourselves of the love we think we deserve. Such behavior only results in a self-righteousness that Jesus singles out as the obstacle to hearing the good news of God's love. We pronounce a judgment against ourselves when we refuse to accept divine love as the only true source of worth.

Not until we surrender to this deepest truth about ourselves will we be able to accept ourselves as reflections of the love of God. We must learn to rely totally on being supported by a love that comes to us out of its own abundance and not out of our own efforts. If we can do so, then we won't have to move through life feeling bad about ourselves. Rather than making our mistakes the measure of our worth, we can accept having shortcomings as an ordinary part of life. If we really believe that we are created in the image of a loving God, then we can free ourselves of misperceptions about who we are. This freedom in turn can give us the energy to improve the quality of our pastoral relationships and to have the interior strength to challenge any structures that continue to erode the self-esteem of others. One of the signs of people with solid self-esteem is their peacefulness. No matter how chaotic the environment around them, they stand as a kind of emotional and spiritual oasis. Since they are not preoccupied with what others think of them and are not being held down by negative images, they can direct their non-defensive energy toward the relationships at hand.

To acquire such a positive self-image, we all need to find ways to reinforce the fundamental biblical insight that we are made in the image of God and that God loves us. Yet, whom do we let name us? To whom do we feel we really belong? Among all the voices trying to claim us, to whom do we listen? Before Jesus began his public ministry, he was tempted by seductive voices promising power, popularity, and security (Matt 4:1-11). He was able to resist these temptations because he allowed himself to be claimed by the voice at the center of his heart that named him and defined his mission. He believed in the word of divine love and lived by its liberating power. But in our world that constantly compares, it is hard to believe that there is a love that does not do the same. In a culture that raises trophy children and runs on ranks and scores, it is hard to believe that there is a love that does not measure us one against another.

At some point in our life, we have to recognize how we have confused God's love for us with the brokenness projected onto us by parents or others whose conditional love masqueraded as caring. For some of us, only therapy will help us rework distorted images of ourselves and of God that have destroyed our self-esteem or are at least eating away at it. For others, perhaps smiles of recognition or kind words of affirmation are enough to build up self-esteem. But none of us will ever come to experience ourselves as being a gift of God's love unless someone values us. To say to another "God loves you" without being the sacramental carrier of that love only makes grace an empty promise. The only way to give another person the experience of grace (of being loved by God) is to treat them graciously. The sacramental principle tells us that human love communicates much more than the simple care of one person for another. It assures us in faith that the tendrils of human love sink deep into the depths of divine love. So let's not be quick to write off as a fluke anyone who has treated us like a treasure. These are revelations of the love of God.

But in our quest for healthy self-esteem, we do not want to become so inflated with our own goodness that we fall into a false perfectionism and deny any capacity for evil in ourselves. We don't have to look far to see how our lives are a tangled web of good and evil. The uncanny insight of my five-year-old niece revealed this basic truth. I asked her once what color she would be if all good people in the world were painted blue and all the bad people were painted yellow. She thought for a moment and then, in her typical matter-of-fact way, said, "I'd be streaky." She caught what is true about us all. We are all streaky.

In the depths of our hearts we will always be doing battle with conflicting tendencies. Even with good self-esteem, we will not lose our capacity to sin, we will still feel some self-doubt, and we will still have to hear some hard truths about how we are not as good as we might think we are. But a healthy self-esteem will not let these dark forces crush us. With the confidence that God's love sustains us and accepts us even when we do not feel very loveable, we can affirm our inclinations to good and feel secure enough to curb our bad ones.

Enhancing self-esteem is the spiritual challenge of accepting God's love and our divine likeness as the source of our worth. To build self-esteem, then, it is helpful to develop spiritual practices that open us to our blessings. One such practice is to meditate on positive biblical stories and images that help us hear the voice of divine love speak to us words of our worth. Listening to the words spoken to Jesus at his baptism as words spoken to us can be a beginning. Other texts can come from those prophets who assure us of how precious we are: "Do not fear. . . . I have called you by name, you are mine. . . . You are precious in my sight. . . . I love you. . . . Do not fear, for I am with you" (Isa 43:1-5); and texts assuring us that God will never abandon us: "Can a woman forget her nursing child? . . . yet I will not forget you. . . . See, I have inscribed you on the palms of my hands" (Isa 49:15-16) and "How can I give you up . . . ?" (Hos 11:8). St. Paul's letter to the Romans is a clear affirmation that nothing can separate us from the love of God: "For I am convinced that neither death nor life, nor angels nor rulers, nor things present, nor things to come, nor powers, nor height, nor depth, nor anything else in all creation, will be able to separate us from the love of God in Christ Jesus our Lord" (Rom 8:38-39). If we can take these words to heart and fill our imaginations with images of being loved by God, then we will be on the way to a healthy self-concept and the liberating love that follows in its wake.

Some other practices that nurture self-esteem through appropriate self-care are these:

- making a periodic life review to clarify values, to recall successes, and to bring to mind people whom we have cherished and who have cherished us;
- maintaining good physical health by getting enough sleep, eating nourishing foods that keep weight down and energy up, follow a regular exercise plan, enjoy leisure time, hobbies, and retreats;
- creating a place for beauty by enjoying the arts, the outdoors, and reflective reading;
- keeping our living space bright, clean, and cheerful with flowers, plants, and mementos;
- making time for friends;
- finding ways to laugh.

These, then, are four virtues for developing humanly. The holiness of pastoral ministers does not grow in a vacuum, but requires a solid basis in these human virtues. In gratitude, we live grateful for grace; with humility, we remain down-to-earth about who we are and what we can do; in fidelity, we foster relationships within boundaries that safeguard everyone's vulnerabilities; and, by assuming responsibility for ourselves through appropriate self-care, we give thanks for being a reflection of divinity itself. With these virtues as a necessary foundation on which grace builds, we can become clearer signs of God's presence in the world and more effective agents of God's love.

# 3

# Developing Spiritually

The second area of ministerial formation is developing spiritually. It has to do with our search for God, our being with or experiencing God, our love of God, and our mediating the presence of God. As I said in the last chapter, the moral and spiritual life begins with grace—God makes the first move. To paraphrase the famous quote of Pascal, we would not be seeking God in our spiritual quest and moral journey if God had not already planted the seeds of this holy longing within us, imprinting the Holy Spirit on our spirit. Theologians see this imprinting as giving us the capacity to be in relationship with something more than ourselves. Without rejecting the infused theological virtues of faith, hope, and love that we readily associate with activating the spiritual life, I want to examine three acquired virtues that surround them. Discernment, piety, and humor enable us to express the intrinsic dynamic of self-transcendence that makes us aware of God—the Transcendence that ultimately grounds us.

## Discernment

Discernment is the bridge connecting our belief that God loves us with our moral behavior. Discovering what cooperating with God's love for the world asks of us is the graced exercise of faith seeking to express itself in action. Discernment is a clear example of our aspiration to be holy (to be in loving relation with God) working together with our attempts to be good (to be one who lives in harmony with God's love). Discernment reaches into the heart to find our desire for God and our commitment to cooperate with God's love in all that we do.

For most people who have some background in the Christian spiritual tradition, discernment connotes a process of making a decision, especially a big decision like deciding on a vocation in life. In its narrowest sense, discernment is the fine sense of discrimination between attractive options. It sorts out the conflicting mix of messages from multiple voices within our hearts and from our social worlds to distinguish which are or which are not messages of God in tune with our deeper self.

As a process of making a decision, discernment tests the "spirits," or the "movements of the heart," to detect which ones reflect God-prompted desires. To be out of touch with these desires is to be out of touch with the Holy Spirit, for the spiritual tradition of the discernment of spirits has understood these murmurings of the heart as God's way of connecting human desires with the Holy Spirit. Discernment treats these heart murmurs, or inner movements of affection, often called "consolation" and "desolation," as surer guides to the deepest truth about ourselves than are the thoughts or ideas going on in our head. The goal of discernment is to discover the most fitting ways to express what our relationship to God demands of us so that we keep our lives in line with our deepest desire for God.

But in naming discernment as one of the special virtues, or habits of the heart, in the spirituality of pastoral ministers, I am not going to pursue the *process* of discerning spirits any further. My interest is to examine discernment on the *inside*: What does it look like as part of the discerning minister's character? What kind of person is a discerning minister? What skills do we need so that we can become discerning ministers?

The outstanding characteristic of discerning ministers is that they are "spirit persons" for the community. These are the people we recognize as "holy" because they make us feel that we are in touch with a special presence that is more than themselves. When we are with them, we feel like we are on holy ground. They relate to us from a deeper center in themselves that conveys an attractive, unmistakable inner peace. There is a keen perceptiveness and integrity about them that is inspiring to the rest of us who still wonder whether the truths we proclaim in our faith are really true. The spirit person lives as though they are.

The religious leaders of all the great religions are like this and so are our saints. When the gospels say of Jesus that he spoke with an authority unlike the religious leaders of his day, they are speaking of him as a "spirit person."[1] What is at stake here is that Jesus spoke from his own experience of God rather than in footnotes from the tradition. He lived in the presence of God and mediated that sacred presence through his words and deeds in unmistakable clarity. That's what spirit persons do. They live with a strong sense that there is more to reality than meets the eye in ordinary experience, and they bring us into relationship with what they know firsthand. This is the basic characteristic of discerning ministers. Most of us are still trying to realize it. When we meet someone who has it, we can't miss it. The vitality and energy of the Spirit in them is too palpable to deny. We know we want more of it. We want to be in touch with what has touched them.

Being a spirit person represents the fullest expression of the virtue of discernment. While becoming a spirit person may be more gift than achievement, all of us can share in something of what it takes. Two skills stand out as necessary dimensions of being a discerning minister: hearing and seeing.

Hearing is the skill of attentive listening. When I have asked participants in my workshops to name their three most important virtues for pastoral ministry, "listening" is often on their list. While they describe listening as the pastoral art of empathic understanding, I also hear in this an intuitive grasp of discernment as the governing virtue for which listening is one of the core skills.

"Pay attention!" is the fundamental imperative for discernment. It applies to hearing and to seeing. In matters of discernment, everything depends on our ability to pay attention to what is going on within us and without us. To do so we need both a rational and an emotional intelligence.[2] Listening within requires that we pay attention to feelings, intuitions, dreams, and somatic reactions.[3] Listening without requires that we pay attention to what is going on in our local community and in the wider world.

The skill of listening to the deeper levels of the self requires that we become comfortable with the language of the heart. The unconscious, affective, intuitive, and somatic dimensions of ourselves are valid ways of recognizing what is true but different from the ways our rational mind works. The discerning minister learns to trust these nonrational ways of knowing and lets them have their say, if not as the last word, then at least as a significant word in our conscious decision making. In fact, the unconscious, the intuitive, and the somatic reactions respond to our experiences more quickly and sensitively than does our rational analysis. We know in our affections, our dreams, our hunches, and in our bodies before we know in our minds what way of life fits who we are and what we must do. Physical symptoms of distress and chronic discomfort, for example, are often clear signs that we are going against our own truth, whereas a body that is in harmony is often a reliable sign that we are on the right path. Furthermore, our emotions and intuitions give us an initial interpretation of our experience before we begin to reflect on it. They alert us to subtle nuances in the situation that disinterested, detached reason can miss. They also help us recognize the particular and personal response that fits us in this situation.

But we need to be critical of these nonrational ways of knowing too. While they can communicate their own insights, they can also perpetuate their own prejudices. For example, we might experience an uneasy feeling about the direction a pastoral relationship is going, such as in a spiritual direction relationship. That "uneasiness" doesn't necessarily mean that we have crossed a boundary to redefine the relationship as an amorous one. When we step back to understand our emotional reaction from a critical, rational perspective, we may see that this funny feeling is coming from a necessary transference by the directee. It is not a sign of crossing boundaries that will redefine the relationship. While we need to respect uneasy feelings and other "reasons of the heart" for the personal dimensions of experience they open to us, we need to remember their potential to mislead. Reliable discernment is never purely an emotional or intuitive conclusion; but neither is it purely logical. The critical mind and the sensitive heart must work together to inform and check each other. Discernment is both affective and cognitive at the same time.

Discernment is not only listening *to* our hearts but also listening *with* our hearts to what is going on in the world around us. Listening with our hearts to others is the beginning of orienting ourselves toward compassion and justice, two virtues of the pastoral dimension of ministry. My favorite example of such heartfelt listening is in Arthur Miller's play, *Death of a Salesman*. Willy Loman's wife, Linda, aware of Willy's eroding self-confidence, pleads the case of her desperate husband with their son, Biff, who has lost all respect for his father. Linda says,

> Biff, I don't say he's a great man. Willy Loman never made a lot of money. His name was never in the paper. He's not the finest character that ever lived. But he's a human being, and a terrible thing is happening to him. So attention must be paid. He's not to be allowed to fall into his grave like an old dog. Attention, attention must be finally paid to such a person.[4]

She knows that anyone who goes unnoticed not only feels invisible but actually falls out of the picture. Paying attention with the heart bestows the blessing of being recognized as someone worthy of love. But listening with sensitivity is not as easy as it seems. It is a real asceticism. Perhaps that is why the Buddha said, "Don't just do something, stand there." When we stand there attentively we can make a conscious, deliberate effort to let what is before us make its impact on us.

Seeing is the second skill of a discerning minister. It is closely intertwined with hearing. Seeing is the capacity for perception and imagination. It is looking beneath the surface to get a glimpse of the mystery of life beyond what meets the eye. A spirit person sees this way and connects with the mystery of God reaching out to us beneath the surface of the ordinary experience and inviting a response. We believe that God is present in our world, but we do not always have the evidence we would like in order to confirm the presence of God. We will not see the divine dimension of life if we remain detached observers. Not until we become involved in the life of faith will we be attuned to the divine presence as a "felt" sense. We have such a felt sense at those times when we are "struck by" or "moved by" the mysterious dimension of experience. We know there is something more than meets the eye. Only in faith do we see these movements linking us to God as the source of our lives, animating, empowering, and renewing us. For the spirit person, the world of experience speaks of God's presence. The spirit person sees God in more and more places in life and links to God all that makes up life.

Seeing is also a capacity of the imagination. How we exercise our ministry is greatly influenced not only by what we see going on but also by what we envision as possible in response. Attentiveness reorients our way of thinking, judging, and acting. Through the imagination we can walk around inside the world of another person and discover ways to communicate our empathic understanding. Without the imagination we would not be able to see beyond present reality to envision a new order of relationships in a situation that might otherwise appear to have no exit. This skill of seeing imaginatively has allowed some pastoral ministers to create a new order for their communities. Some have envisioned men and women working together, the ordained and the non-ordained, in shared collegial responsibility and have designed organizational structures to suit. Others have found ways for celibate priests living alone to share a residence and still serve their respective communities.

The Good Samaritan parable (Luke 10:25-37) is a good example of how attentive listening can join with an empathic imagination to bring about a response in line with the dream of God. Because he pays attention, the Samaritan sees through social divisions to a relationship of solidarity. The sight of the man beaten and lying abandoned in the ditch shocks his imagination with a fresh image of what being neighbor means. By paying attention to his heartfelt response to what he sees, the Samaritan is able to expand his vision of inclusive love. Similarly, to the extent that we cooperate with God's love living within us, or grace, we can help one another to live in justice and peace. Cooperating with divine love means that we continually call into question and seek to reform oppressive and dominating structures in society and in the church so that everyone can live in a community of equal respect and mutual concern. Such action represents the social dimension of being a discerning minister.

It follows, then, that discerning ministers can educate themselves about their social world by asking: What is going on? Why are things that way? What forces and factors keep them that way? Taking a close look at some very upsetting realities with even these modest questions of social analysis enables us to figure out how best to use our energy and resources to respond to social needs. Working with others, we too hope to bring the social situation in line with the dream of God—a vision of the world where people do not hurt or destroy, oppress or exploit, but cooperate in serving the common good.[5]

How do we know that what we hear when we pay attention is actually God's invitation and not mere ego projection? This depends a great deal on how well tuned our ears are to the call of God. William Spohn offers this illuminating analogy to express what is required:

> A piano tuner ought to know how to read music, strike the keys on the keyboard, work the pedals, and be able to tighten or loosen the piano strings to produce true notes. None of these skills will help if she does not have a good ear for pitch. The criterion for tuning pianos is internal. Only a very ac-

curate sense of pitch will tell whether the notes being sounded are true or off. The skill lies in registering harmony so acutely that the slightest deviation is detected.[6]

In a similar way, to be a spirit person requires an "ear" for God, or a keen religious sense that has internalized the "mind of Christ." To develop such an ear requires sufficient faith and personal maturity that would enable us to have a sense of who God is, of how God acts in our lives, and of who we are. If we do not yet have faith enough to be open to the presence of God in the depth of human experience, or if we lack the self-possession to direct our lives intentionally or to speak truth to power when necessary, or if we swing from one mood to another in a world of emotional uncertainty, or if we are not yet free enough to care about others and to commit ourselves to their well-being, then we are not ready to discern no matter how refined our reasoning mind might be. Without faith, self-possession, emotional stability, and freedom for others, our perception is unlikely to be true.

The minister's character is crucial to having confidence that we are hearing the voice of God, for character gives a "connatural" knowledge for what fits our well-patterned inclinations. Connatural knowledge reminds us that, while we can reach a correct judgment by the right use of reason, there is another way. It is by way of the heart, or the emotional resonance between one's own being and what needs to be done. In chapter 1, I used the example of Ernest Shackleton selecting volunteers for the mission of the *Endurance* bound for Antarctica to illustrate the close connection between character and connaturality. The resonance of connaturality is like the knowledge a lover has of the beloved, or a mother of her child. Someone who is disposed to be compassionate, for example, knows to do the comforting thing without being instructed to do it. Shackleton's experience as a seaman gave him a keen sense of who could endure his mission without having to interview them at length. Similarly, the honest person spots deception quickly; the manipulative person finds ways to be deceptive without any effort. While character is crucial to this way of knowing, not just any type of character will do for discerning life in the Spirit. To have a soulful connection with God's desires for us requires a fundamental commitment to be disposed to know and love God. The more we have this built-in "homing device" for God, the greater will be the possibility of discerning the call of God in the situation.

Accompanying an "ear" for God and a character committed to knowing and loving God is the presupposition that we have also experienced discernment. That is, we have been through the prayerful process of experiencing the different "spirits"; we have learned to reflect on them, especially with the help of a spiritual friend, and we have patiently tested them over time. In this process, we have learned to live with conflicting attitudes: we want to trust our feelings, but we remember how easily they can mislead us; we believe that God speaks through human experience, yet we are wary of the ambiguity of experience. Along with personally working through conflicts like these, we must also be willing and able to communicate our experiences in prayer to others in ways that reveal our sense of God's guidance without grandstanding ourselves.

Since discernment is the process of interpreting the affective movements evoked by our experiences and by imaginatively engaging ways to respond to God's presence, it requires some "downtime" and the discipline of sitting still and being quiet enough to hear the voice of God beneath the surface noise of our life.[7] We cannot hear God's invitation if we are caught up in the hustle and bustle of hectic activity or subject to physical distress or chaotic emotions that obscure or confuse God's call to us. So that the voices within and without can present themselves with God's support, this downtime must be spent in the context of faith. Prayer provides that space. The prayer of discernment is first of all an attitude of openness to God's presence and a willingness to listen so that we can hear the call of God. Moreover, prayerful openness to what is going on inside us and around us is a way to free ourselves from external pressures and selfish preferences that fix our hearts in advance on one particular way of responding.

Prayerful listening seeks the interior freedom that leaves us open to God's call. Achieving this freedom is not easy. So many attachments or illusions compete to enslave our hearts, such as our fear of change, peer pressure, status, anxieties, and the need for control. A regular rhythm of prayerful listening, along with good physical and emotional health, and sometimes the guidance of a wise helper, may be the key to unlocking our imaginations and letting go of all that wants to prevent us from hearing God's call.

We confirm our contact with the Holy Spirit and know that we are becoming spirit persons not by the criteria of strict logic, but by the aesthetic criterion of a deep feeling of inner peace and harmony, warmth in our relationships, and energy for our mission. In the end, the movement toward God finds its external expression in the steady desire to love God and to love our neighbor as ourselves.

Some practices that nurture discernment:

- standing there, before doing something;
- taking some downtime;
- sitting still and being quiet;
- reflecting back on the day and notice where you have felt most alive;
- naming the feelings that have marked your day;
- praying imaginatively with a Scripture text to feel the encounter with Christ;
- watching the daily news and imagining yourself in another's world;
- taking a long, loving look at a pressing social condition;
- sharing experiences of prayer with a trusted friend.

## Piety

The discussion of the virtue of discernment already introduced us to piety in upholding the important role of spiritual practices to school the heart for discernment. Piety is our spiritual address. To live a spiritual life, we all need a place where we can be addressed by God and where we can address God. Piety is where God can reach us, where we can be at home with God, and where we relate to God in our most personal ways. In short, piety is how we show our love for God.

For believers, loving God is not only the fundamental imperative governing the moral life but also our primary spiritual act. After all, if spirituality is about our relation to God, then whatever we do to show our love for God and deepen this relationship is integral to our spirituality. Just as no friendship could be sustained if friends do not spend time together, neither could we sustain a relationship with God if we did not take time to focus our attention on that relationship. For this reason, I contend that we really do not have a spiritual life without a commitment to spiritual practices. That is, we need to have some form of devotional life that expresses our love for God in ways other than by loving our neighbors. Loving God cannot be reduced to loving our neighbor. Devotional practices, or spiritual disciplines, are fundamentally acts of worship that show our love for God apart from loving our neighbor.

Edward Vacek has carefully drawn out the distinction between love of God and love of neighbor to support the role of the virtue of piety in the spiritual life. We know that lovers are inclined to love what the beloved loves, and so we readily jump to the conclusion that loving God means loving our neighbor, without ever stopping to savor the value of being alone with God for the sake of the relationship. When reformulating the love command by combining the two classic Old Testament texts about love of God (Deut 6:4-5) and love of neighbor (Lev 19:18), Jesus distinguished but did not separate the relationship to God and relationship to neighbor (Mark 12:28-34). Failing to honor the distinction by making these two loves one and the same is idolatry. Our neighbor is not God. The unity of the two loves must not obscure their difference. While loving God does include loving our neighbor, Vacek argues that these loves need not be identical. We ought not to collapse the whole of what we mean by loving God into neighbor love. If we did, then we would fail to appreciate the value of being in love with God quite apart from loving our neighbor. As Vacek shows, sometimes we must love God "alone" just for the sake of our relation to God.[8] Piety is the virtue that allows us to do that.

But piety, an ancient and perfectly good religious term for a virtue, has become so bruised and battered by mishandling that few, if any, want to own it as a virtue. Just the mention of this term turns people's minds off like a switch. Others wonder why anyone who wants to promote spiritual practices would continue using it. Today we would rather say that we want to deepen our spiritual life, or we are striving to be holy. But pious? No way. To modern ears, piety is met more with scorn than approval. It is taken as a pejorative term characterizing simpletons laboring under naïve notions of God and of how God acts, or hypocrites like those Jesus warned us not to imitate for their insincerity and pretension (Matt 6:1-18). It comes as no surprise, then, that no one in my informal surveys of ministerial groups has ever used "piety" as a necessary virtue for ministers. The closest they have come is to speak of "prayerfulness."

The richer sense of piety includes both the realm of heartfelt devotions to show our love for God as well as our humble commitment to love our neighbor, though some may want to reserve this form of love for charity. Piety as a virtue is neither a stifling moral perfectionism nor a holier-than-thou attitude. As a virtue, it is a profound reverence, awe, and perduring faithfulness to God arising from our own acceptance of God's love as the love on which we are absolutely dependent.[9] Piety brings together not only our love for God, but also other virtues, such as our humility in living dependent on God, our gratitude for the gift-dimension of our lives, and our generosity and compassion in the ways that we cherish others who make up our lives.

Piety in the pastoral minister does not set us on a pedestal above everyone else. As a virtue, it is the way we give witness to our relationship to God as the most important one in our life. We focus on this central relationship, celebrate it, and deepen it through a whole array of devotional practices that usually include those activities we associate with "going to church." They take some form of talking to God, listening to God, or simply being in the presence of God. Devotional activities such as prayer, inspirational reading, meditating on the Bible, celebrating the sacraments, eucharistic adoration (Benediction), praying the Liturgy of the Hours (the Divine Office, or Breviary), reciting litanies, the rosary, or making the Stations of the Cross are all forms of expressing the virtue of piety.

In the first chapter, I already touched on some of the important aspects of piety when treating spiritual practices as a way of practicing the faith. I want to review a few of these themes for what they can add to our understanding of piety as the virtue of loving God.

The first thing about piety is that it gives us a way to be at home with God. It creates a space in our lives where we can focus ourselves on being with God and where God can be with us. God, however, is always a gift; none of us can conjure God up through our pious practices. But through these spiritual practices we make ourselves vulnerable to God and available. As one retreatant pithily put it about her relation to God, "I go into the chapel. Sit still, and say, 'Okay God, I'm here. It's your move.'" The key to exercising piety is to make it an intentional and physical activity that we do on a regular basis in order to express and deepen our relationship with God. The operative terms here are intentional, physical, and God.

As an intentional act, piety is a deliberate effort to relate to God. Rooted in the deep desire of the human heart to be in union with God, we exercise our piety with an openness to receive God's love and to respond to it. As intentional, our piety is neither an occasional burst of enthusiasm nor a duty we perform under the supervision of someone else's watchful eye or in obedience to their command. As physical, it is an exercise that we set time aside to do on a regular basis, like going to church on Sunday, beginning each day with fifteen minutes of quiet prayer, or making a weekly examination of conscience.

In addition, piety is directed to God. Keeping our focus on relating to God helps us understand why we are engaging in these practices in the first place. We do them to show our love for God and to open ourselves to God's love. We do not engage in these practices of piety primarily to improve our life or to orient us toward loving our neighbor. While there may be a moral dimension to our spiritual practices, this dimension is an indirect effect of the practice. Primarily, we are loving God, being with God, deepening our awareness of God, and creating space to allow God to address us. William Spohn is emphatic on this point: "If the intent of worship is not God but personal growth, then God is being reduced to a means, which is a form of idolatry."[10]

When engaged with the right intention, piety is our personal way of expressing our faith in accepting God's love for us and expressing our desire to love God. Some practices that cultivate and express piety are:

- participating in the communal prayer of the church;
- taking time for quiet to fill our senses with the presence of God;
- developing a regular discipline of some devotional practice, such as *lectio divina*;
- learning about the classics of spirituality so that our piety may be grounded in sound understanding;
- living a simple lifestyle of self-sacrifice.

### Humor

Humor is my third virtue for the spiritual dimension of pastoral ministry. A sense of humor is a sign of a resurrection faith and life in the Spirit. Among those whom I admire for their spiritual life, and those who have served as models for developing these virtues, I find a common denominator in their ability to laugh (and to get me to laugh with them). Their sense of humor (or humor, for short) makes their spirituality visible, tangible, and infectious. What sets them apart is not their ability to tell jokes, since not all can, but their ability to catch mismatched events in life, to laugh at themselves, and to take themselves with only as much seriousness as the situation deserves. They have taught me that humor as a virtue is not about trying to be a comedian doing stand-up. Rather, having a sense of humor is about perceiving discrepancies and incongruities in daily life, about embracing absurdities in human experience without granting them the last word. Humor enables us to let go of control and to sit more lightly on life by not taking ourselves too seriously.

To regard humor as a virtue may seem odd to some, especially to those who have been hurt by humor. We can all probably recall instances where someone was victimized by biting humor, sarcasm, racist, ethnic, or sexist jokes that belittle and dehumanize. How could humor be a virtue when it can be so vicious and cut so deeply? While humor can be used to put down, its positive aspects can raise up, cheer up, restore perspective, and bring vitality to an otherwise somber spirituality.

Humor as a virtue is grounded in the same conviction that grounds the other virtues—God is beneficent and sustains us in love. This is our foundational conviction shaping our perspective on what is going on. The beneficence of God is our normal. A sense of humor requires some grasp of what is normal so that we can judge something funny because it doesn't fit what we would take to be the way things should be.[11] We know from trying to tell a joke that we can only be successful if both we and our audience share the same assumptions about what is normal. If we don't have an implicitly shared background, we will miss the punch line that should evoke a laugh because, in revealing the unexpected, it reverses what should be.

Humor is a Christian virtue when the conviction that God loves us and wants what is good for us is the backdrop against which we are able to see the oddities in human experience. Pastoral ministers who take seriously their role of helping people through hard times are going to need a sense of humor, if only to point out how far the world falls from "normal." We may strike a note of hope if we can read the signs of the times against our fundamental conviction that God is for us. Humor helps us to move forward with hope that the world can run better than it is.

Some, however, may still feel that humor has no place in religion because trading on the majesty of God is serious business. They can even find some support for this disposition in the empirical studies that have been done to show how religion mistrusts humor.[12] Such an attitude gets reinforced by the way some church leaders are depicted in the news media. Such images and reports confirm in the popular mind the idea that religion is deadly serious and humor is unbecoming for anyone who deals in the sphere of the divine.

Religion's suspicion of humor was brought home to a general reading audience several years ago in Umberto Eco's novel, *The Name of the Rose*.[13] In this medieval mystery tale, the monk Jorge the librarian poisoned the pages of the one book in the monastery that proposed God laughed so that anyone who licked his thumb after turning the page would die. Jorge thought that humor would bring God down to our level of weakness and make God involved in the foolishness of the flesh. Jorge is an example of those who feel that we really only find God in suffering, never in joy. Humor for the likes of Jorge is inconsistent with the elegance of God and the dignity of those who minister in God's name.

But if we don't have a sense of humor, then we are going to miss how much of our faith is filled with paradoxes such as the gospel proclamations that the weak inherit the earth, the foolish shame the wise, the lame are restored to wholeness, becoming like a child is the sign of greatness, a virgin gives birth, a king is born in a stable, and God takes on human nature. Then comes the most unexpected ending of all. In rising from the dead, the crucified Christ has the last laugh over death and the forces of evil. Easter fulfills the aphorism, "Whoever laughs last laughs best." Humor, joy, laughter are all signs of the positive outlook that characterizes resurrection faith in the power of life over death and love over hatred. If accepting the incongruities within the kerygma as true doesn't require a sense of humor, then I don't know what does.

We can so easily turn the affairs of the church into grim realities. The temptation is to become weighted down with gravity of matter and to treat prayer and worship with excessive formality and still call it a "celebration." Sometimes, the best thing we can say to those under our care is "lighten up," "get real," "you're only human." Teresa of Avila warned her cloistered nuns that a sad nun is a bad nun. That takes a sense of humor.

So I ask you, amid the grim realities of the church, do we have enough lightness to offset the heaviness? For example, we often hear it said that the shortage of priests is a great crisis. For some, it threatens our sacramental life. For others, it is an opportunity to let lay ministries emerge. At least that is how this one lay minister saw it. As the story goes, she was seated at the banquet table waiting for the festivity to begin when the president of the parish council realized that the priest has not yet arrived to give the invocation. The president whispered to her, "Since Father hasn't come, will you give the blessing?" She rose, bowed her head, and with deep feeling said, "There being no priest present, let us thank God." When we who are involved in the church start to take ourselves too seriously, then it is time to recall Pope John XXIII's remark to the journalist who asked him how many people work in the Vatican. Pope John replied, "About half." Now there's a pastoral leader with a sense of humor!

Mark Twain once said that "humor is mankind's greatest blessing." In worlds outside of religion we are already meeting some of these blessings, especially in the holistic health movement. It includes laughter as a healing remedy. Norman Cousins popularized laughter as good medicine in his bestseller, *Anatomy of an Illness*, where he recounts how he experienced the analgesic effects of hearty laughter. After watching segments of Alan Funt's program *Candid Camera* and some old Marx Brothers films, Cousins concludes:

It worked. I made the joyous discovery that ten minutes of genuine belly laughter has an anesthetic effect and would give me at least two hours of pain-free sleep. When the pain-killing effect of the laughter wore off, we would switch on the motion-picture projector again, and, not infrequently, it would lead to another pain-free sleep interval. Sometimes, the nurse read to me out of a trove of humor books. Especially useful were E. B. and Katherine White's *Subtreasury of American Humor* and Max Eastman's *The Enjoyment of Laughter*.[14]

Later in the book he remarks, "What was significant about the laughter . . . was not just the fact that it provides internal exercise for a person flat on his or her back—a form of jogging for the innards—but that it creates a mood in which the other positive emotions can be put to work, too. In short, it helps make it possible for good things to happen."[15]

Other studies have reported how humor can reduce the impact of stress by helping us cope better. Humor gives us the ability to absorb adverse experiences in life; it mitigates depression, and it helps the disabled develop an outlook that makes their misfortune more bearable.[16] From all of these studies, it is safe to conclude that in the world of physical and emotional health, good humor and hearty laughter can relieve tension, heal, restore balance by bringing in joy and fun to offset sadness and misery, and even help us to take the inevitable bumps in the road more creatively.

Since a sense of humor grounds us in our humanity and enhances it, and since there is no dichotomy between being human and being spiritual, then humor has a fitting place within our spirituality. Its self-transcending capacity relativizes our importance by taking the focus off us and returning it to God. This feature of humor is supported by sociologist Peter Berger's notion of humor as a "signal of transcendence."[17] Berger describes humor as an aspect of human experience that points to something beyond us that is real. In religious terms, we would say that humor manifests a sacramental universe. It is a visible sign of an invisible reality. Humor is a sign of God's presence. By pointing to a divine reality at the deeper dimensions of human experience, humor allows us to relativize the oddities in our human condition.

In the perspective of resurrection faith, laughing at the incongruities we face from day to day makes life easier to bear, at least briefly, because we believe that the miseries we know now do not ultimately define our destiny. As the Eucharistic Prayer for Children reads, "One day . . . / there will be no more suffering, / no more tears, no more sadness." Humor takes the onus off our shoulders to have to make everything turn out right. By lightening our load, it gives us the freedom to act now as if the redemption that is yet to come in its fullness is already here. As a result, we can sit more lightly on life, not take our finite experiences as though they had eternal importance, and let go of needing to be in absolute control as though we were masters of the universe. With a sense of humor we can see beyond the limits of our everydayness to the ultimate redemption still unfolding and let God be God.

Humor also assists us with the virtue of discernment in the way it sharpens our capacity for perception, the ability to distinguish what fits and what doesn't.[18] While there is no consensus on a comprehensive theory for what makes something funny among philosophers and psychologists who have analyzed humor, there is one recurring theme: humor is based on incongruity. What they mean by this is that those who have a sense of humor are able to perceive that one thing is mismatched with another. For example, what makes the following funny?

> "Why do croutons come in airtight packages? Aren't they just stale bread to begin with?"
>
> "If it's true that four out of five people suffer from diarrhea, does that mean one enjoys it?"
>
> "A balanced diet is having chocolate in both hands."

We find these lines funny because we catch the incongruity between matching stale bread with the freshness we would expect of food in a vacuum sealed package; we catch the play on "suffering" to mean "feeling miserable" in one instance but simply "having an experience" in the other; and we catch the mismatched use of "balance" suggesting, on the one hand, two sides of a scale in equilibrium with, on the other hand, a "balanced" diet that means a nutrition plan that contains more than one item from a single food group. We can laugh at these incongruities because we have the discerning perception to catch the meaning that doesn't fit.

Similarly, we can also laugh with Erma Bombeck's title *I Lost Everything in the Post-Natal Depression* because we know that the period of economic decline when many people lost all of their savings is not the same "depression" as the medical condition after giving birth. Oscar Wilde's comment, "Life is much too important to be taken seriously," strikes us as too wild to be true because we associate important things with seriousness. We find all of these statements funny because our perception is catching what doesn't fit. The virtue of discernment needs a sense of humor to keep our perception sharp so that we can catch the distinctions that truly make a difference.

Humor is also aligned with humility to keep us grounded in our humanity. If humility is the virtue of being down-to-earth about ourselves, then humor and humility are hitched at the hip as inseparable siblings. Humility nudges us to face up to the truth about ourselves, not to take ourselves too seriously, and frees us to laugh at ourselves. Not to be able to laugh at the claims we make on the situations we face narrows our vision of the world and skews our sense of justice toward self-centeredness. But having a sense of humor about our unrealistic expectations for ourselves or others brings us down to earth where we can be at home again with our own vulnerability. That is why we can laugh when we hear Rodney Dangerfield say, "My wife and I were happy for twenty years; then we met." And we can appreciate the utter humanity of Mae West's confession, "I used to be Snow White; then I drifted." When we are with someone who is able to laugh at himself or herself, we know how quickly we feel at ease with ourselves as well. Their perspective is contagious; their laughter infectious. We begin to laugh too.

In the realm of religion and pastoral ministry, the temptation is to be excessively formal. Humor aligned with humility allows us to lighten up, to let go of the order we have imposed on reality as the only way life has to be, to bring God back to center stage, and to be open to something new. Humor also helps us face difficult moments with some creativity, as in this instance. The pastor announced at the end of Mass that he was being transferred to another parish. After seven years of tension, conflict, and division within the community, he was finally moving on. He told the congregation that the same Jesus who called him to this place was the Jesus now calling him to another. Then he stepped down from the pulpit. All were silent. The choir director motioned for the assembly to rise and join in singing their final hymn, "What a Friend We Have in Jesus."

Humor cultivates relationships, too, because laughter has the power to draw people into closer bonds of community. Laughing together satisfies a deep human longing to be connected. No wonder public speakers like to begin with a few jokes. The disarming quality of humor enables a connection with and among the audience. We are building on this same quality of laughter when we pass on a good joke that we have heard, even when we pass it on over the internet so that we can laugh together in cyberspace. If the spiritual life is relational and friends are indispensable to spiritual growth, then we need to surround ourselves with friends who dispose us to laugh. I am lucky to have friends like that. One in particular is well known for his humor, especially his jokes. "Have you heard the one about . . ." is his signature sentence fragment. When he walks into a room everyone begins to smile even before he speaks. We know what's coming. He will get us to laugh, often at ourselves, and this always draws us closer together. If we can laugh first at ourselves, then we can liberate ourselves from an alienating narcissism and become better companions. When we laugh together we build bonds of community. Humor allows us to accept the limitations of our shared humanity, to reconcile with being human, and to live with the absurdities by keeping them in proper perspective.

The evidence seems clear—good humor and hearty laughter can relieve tension, be healing, give us perspective, and help us take the inevitable bumps in the road more creatively. So when life in the church starts to get heavy and grim, spend time with people who have a sense of humor and who can laugh at themselves. Take a laugh break, along with your coffee break. Humor is refreshing too. It is a sign that we are alive in the Spirit.

Some practices that nurture humor:[19]

- looking for the incongruities in Scripture and in everyday life;
- spending time with people who have a sense of humor;
- setting aside time to watch your favorite TV program or a film that makes you laugh;
- taking time to laugh with friends over the mismatched moments of ministry;
- thinking about someone who makes you laugh and get in touch with that person today.

If there is one service that our people rightfully expect us to provide through our ministry, it is to be a spiritual resource for them. The virtues of discernment, piety, and humor are the foundation for opening others to the mystery of God's presence and for showing the way to living in the Spirit of God. Discernment enables us to pay attention to the presence and action of God and to respond to situations in ways that fit our deepest desire for God; piety drives our spiritual practices to give us a place where we can address God and God can reach us; and humor is the self-transcending capacity that allows us to sit lightly on life, to relativize our self-importance, and to keep our focus on God.

# 4

## Developing Intellectually

The third area of development is intellectual. The spirituality of pastoral ministers is intellectual inasmuch as ministers are commissioned to teach, preach, and provide moral guidance, whether formally or informally. Because we interpret experience and culture in light of the gospel and the living tradition of faith, we have great need for wisdom and prudence.

### Wisdom

Of all the virtues being considered for this morally integrated spirituality, wisdom is the most difficult to describe. The others lend themselves more easily to a specific judgment, emotion, or action. Wisdom is more elusive. We associate it better with gurus—Socrates, Confucius, Buddha, Jesus, Gandhi, Black Elk. Through them we see wisdom has much to do with a commitment to truth, especially the truthfulness of what life is all about.

Wisdom as a philosophical commitment to truth has its critics. For St. Paul, God has made the wisdom of the world foolishness, since it has nothing to do with knowing God (1 Cor 1:20-22). Others, however, side with philosophical skeptics to regard any reliance on religious belief for truth to be mere speculation. Then the association of wisdom with intelligence cuts in two directions. A conventional understanding of wisdom says that while "whiz kids" may be geniuses when it comes to theoretical knowledge, they have no clue about what is important in life. Or, there are those who have had very little schooling but are truly wise, for they live with a keen sense of what life requires.

Wisdom as a virtue for a morally integrated spirituality is the desire and the discipline to discover the truth, to reflect on what we learn, and to integrate what we know into our personal experiences so that we can live well with others. To this end, wisdom is the fruit of the confluence of several virtues. It requires the docile spirit of an inquiring mind discovering more and more. It is stifled by complacency, arrogance, shallowness, and triviality. Wisdom is always seeking and yearning to go beyond where we are now to know more about what life requires. It craves more experience, more insight, more love, more understanding. But wisdom is not satisfied with just any experience or insight. It ultimately longs for what is true. In part, wisdom is the fruit of our curiosity about the way the world works, about the mysteries of nature, about what makes individuals tick and societies thrive or decay. It keeps asking, seemingly without end, what is it? and, is it so?

Another part of wisdom is a humble acknowledgment of not knowing. Wisdom implies a critical self-knowledge, especially of one's own ignorance and limits. It also requires fidelity, justice, and compassion, for wisdom is not self-serving. It knows how to fit in with others. Wisdom also requires courage to persevere through the tedious investigation of resources that are sometimes dense and difficult to mine. Against the ever-present temptation to confirm one's own bias, wisdom is continually reflecting on theoretical knowledge and on personal experience by raising critical questions to illuminate a richer understanding of life. Wisdom also implies discernment, for it is able to distinguish what is really important from what only appears to be so. Wisdom grasps the significance of various aspects of life against a larger vision of a good life.

The incarnational nature of Christianity adds another dimension to wisdom. To believe that God has entered the world in Christ directs our search for God, our ultimate Truth, through knowing the created order in its deepest level. That nagging craving for more is a divine invitation to seek what is genuinely fulfilling. Our hunger for God gets disguised in the human longing to know as much as we can about the way things are. Our love for learning extends the reach of our minds to grasp more and more the truth of things, especially how to live well. This search is a manifestation of our love for God and our desire to come to a deeper appreciation for what God has done and continues to do in the world. Nothing short of uniting our craving to know and to love with knowing and loving God will satisfy our hungering spirit.

As twinned as wisdom and ministry might be, however, we still find some resistance to making the search for wisdom an integral part of ministerial spirituality. For some pastoral ministers a prejudice persists that puts a love for learning and critical theological investigation at odds with spirituality. I remember one ministerial student who protested to the dean about having to take courses on critical approaches to the Bible. His argument was that reading the Bible with critical tools would only dry up his prayer life. For him the intellectual work of reading and studying could only compete with and sabotage his spiritual life. Not being willing to do the work necessary to read the Bible intelligently cut short his way to wisdom in biblical matters and disqualified him as a viable candidate for ministry.

For others, the disciplined study that acquiring wisdom requires only distracts from the real work of ministry and from becoming holy. Louis Cameli, when speaking to a gathering of seminary formation personnel, identified two types of candidates whose models of ministry undermine the disciplined work acquiring wisdom requires. One type prizes the value of being pastoral. They want to keep themselves on the same level as those they serve. They do not want their knowledge to set them apart and so they offer a type of ministerial service that does not require the intellectual discipline of critical reflection that leads to the integration of faith and personal experience. It is enough for them to be kind, affirming, encouraging, and to have a knack for understanding the human condition. A second type has an exalted sense of themselves as being set apart from the faithful as ones chosen to act *in persona Christi*. This model does not require much intellectual engagement either. For "wisdom" they only need right information easily accessed from the Bible, the Catechism, or canon law.[1] Neither model prizes wisdom. What counts is feeling over thinking for the first group and being the icon of Christ over critically mediating Christ for the second. Neither seeks to grow in the habit of critical reflection, of discerning judgment, or of integrating the Christian tradition with personal experience.

Another obstacle is the presumption that ministers' ongoing study and reading only leads to complicating matters for people who do not need to know much beyond a basic catechesis. The fear that more learning would only disturb the simple faithful is not only intolerably patronizing but also mistakenly presumes that reducing all matters of faith to their simplest terms is the best service ministry can provide. How many times have we met people who are devout Christians and highly skilled in a secular profession but who have no idea of how to read the Bible critically or to make any connection between going to Mass and doing works of justice? Their faith remains childish, not childlike, for its lack of critical knowledge. When we lack a commitment to further study and fail to cultivate the life of the mind, we remain unable to present the tradition of the church intelligently. Our ministry easily slips into providing second-rate services and we risk losing our educated laity who seek homilies of substance and teaching that connects faith to life.

By contrast, the wise are those for whom a love for learning, with its habit of intellectual practices, has become second nature. We characterize them as wise because we can count on their judgments to be the fruit of critical reflection and personal integration of life's experiences with the mysteries of faith. We hope that ministerial candidates form these habits during their years of study in preparation for ministry. Once acquired, the habit of study nurtures wisdom through the practices of lifelong learning. Brain scientists are telling us how this habit is perfectly in line with the natural capacity of the brain to change in response to new experiences. Becoming a lifelong learner capitalizes on brain plasticity to make wisdom a virtue that can become stronger and stronger. But it is also subject to the law of entropy. Given that wisdom is a habit acquired through repetitive actions, such as study and critical thinking, it can atrophy from lack of practice. The reading and studying that make us lifelong learners and the reflection and integration with life experiences are crucial for nurturing and strengthening wisdom.

We shouldn't expect our seminary training to provide everything we need to know for ministry nor to satisfy our hunger for truth. When seminary education ends, we ought to be prepared well enough to begin serving as an official minister, but the ending of our initial training program is truly a commencement. We have only just begun to learn. Our commitment to ongoing education can take many forms. For some, it will mean returning to an academic setting for studies that will prepare us for a specialized ministry. For others, it will be an occasional course as a part-time student at a nearby college with or without a degree program in mind. For still others, ongoing education will be a sabbatical program that will introduce us to new ideas and updated reading lists. Then there are always the less formal means—book clubs, private reading, and support groups who carry on informal conversations stimulated by provocative articles in popular opinion magazines. The opportunities for learning are many; the excuses not to take advantage of them are few. Other professions make ongoing education a requirement for renewing certification to practice. Ministry has no such structure of accountability. We have to rely on our own passion for learning and our commitment to provide quality service. We must be able to see study as real ministry and a genuine spiritual practice.

Wisdom, like the other virtues, will show itself in our behavior. The behavioral cues of wisdom are the intellectual processes that move us from experience to action. Bernard Lonergan has clarified the dynamic structure of cognitive activity. We begin with experience that takes in data (through reading and observation, for example); then we reflect on this data, ask questions about it and perhaps even discuss it in order to understand what we are experiencing and why it is so; then we weigh the evidence to pass judgment on the truth or falsity of the conclusions we draw from our understanding; finally we make a prudential choice about how to act in light of what we know.[2] The more attentive, intelligent, and reasonable we are, explains Lonergan, the more we will get to know what is really true and minimize the chance of being blinded by our own assumptions and prejudices. For this process to lead us to truth, we need enduring patience and a healthy skepticism that keeps us from jumping too quickly to hasty conclusions. In the end, coming to wisdom requires a willingness to reconsider or abandon our own position in light of new questions and new evidence.

All the intellectual activities that we do as we study can take on the quality of spiritual practices, as they too can open us to God. Simone Weil's famous essay on academic work gives us a way of thinking about how to make the intellectual dimension of ministry integral to spirituality. Her argument focuses not on the content of our learning but on how studying cultivates a capacity for attention (the very capacity that we met in the last chapter at the center of the virtue of discernment). For Weil, pursuing intellectual work is worth sacrificing our time and resources because, even if we don't solve the problem we are investigating, our efforts always have an effect on the spiritual level by increasing our power for attention—a power we must cultivate if we are to pray or be present to others. Moreover, for her, intellectual work is also like a sacrament in that the particular truths we do discover point us to the eternal Truth, which is the ultimate end we are pursuing.[3]

Weil's perspective on the relation of intellectual work to our capacity for attention supports ongoing study as an integral part of ministry. Taking an occasional class as a part-time student, reading, and reflecting on a regular basis are not interruptions to the service we provide but a deepening of the very work of ministry itself. Certainly we can make reading an escape that shelters us from the multiple demands of ministry, and some of our reading should do that. But setting aside a portion of our day or week to read in ways that expand our minds and that help us better understand our faith, our culture, and personal experiences must be integral to ministry. Study is ministry too, and reading can become a fruitful spiritual practice.[4]

Granted, reading is not the only way to acquire wisdom. But reading has certainly proven itself as a reliable way to expand our consciousness and to draw us more deeply into the world and into the life of God. Reading also keeps the ministries of preaching and teaching fresh. Preachers especially must read with others in mind. One of the tasks of preachers is to take what they have learned from study and shape it into images for others to use for understanding and digesting their own experience. Woe is the community that is subjected to a preacher who has stopped reading—who no longer reads the Bible, biblical commentaries, theology, novels, poetry, or magazines with political and cultural commentary. One criticism I hear of preachers is that they lack substance. A critical listener easily spots the difference between reflective preaching and a stale homily, between something rooted in contemplative study and the same old message. The difference turns on whether preachers read and reflect and how widely they read and how much time they give to reflection. So much of our ministry is communicating to others what we have discovered in studying the texts of our faith and of human experience. But staying abreast of developments in theology and in culture is a daunting task. On the information highway, everything moves at warp speed. Where do we find the time? What do we read? No wonder we all complain that we are behind and always playing catch-up. The demands on our time and our human limitations are no match for the superabundance of information now available to us in printed and electronic form. But not being caught up is no excuse for not keeping at it.

To communicate the faith wisely, ministers, especially anyone who dares to preach, must educate themselves as broadly as possible. We need a rich array of resources from which to draw language and images that connect the stories of Jesus and the mysteries of faith to people's deepest questions. Reading for preaching is not only an intellectual discipline but also a spiritual practice. It becomes a place where we meet God through marveling at the wonders of creation and at the complexity of human experience. Through reading we can also imagine creative ways to respond to God by using our resources to make the church a clearer sign and agent of God's action in the world.

Moreover, making wisdom a virtue integral to pastoral ministers fits squarely with our professional role of being a theological resource for the communities we serve. One does not have to be in ministry very long before hearing the cry of the people who want to deepen their spiritual life. While what they mean by this is not always clear, one unmistakable aspect is the desire to make their commitment of faith more than a matter of going to church on Sunday. They want to be able to touch the holy in the everyday events of life, and they want to draw upon their faith to make sense of their experiences, especially the difficult ones whose meaning is hard to fathom. As pastoral ministers, we profess to be able to respond to this religious need, for we are the designated "go-to" person to serve as the theological resource for the believing community. Wisdom is part and parcel of this professional responsibility.

As pastoral ministers, we share with other professionals many skills (counseling, organizing, teaching, active listening, etc.) that are not unique to ministry. But we don't have to be therapists, sociologists, or accountants. Wisdom implies humility—it knows the limits of one's competence. Wisdom is knowing what we don't know so that we do not try to provide services in areas where we lack knowledge and skill. We must be ready to refer our people to other professionals when they need help that we are not trained to give.

Pastoral ministers, in whatever capacity (pastor, chaplain, catechist, youth minister, spiritual director, etc.), bear the distinctive identity and purpose in society of being the dedicated professionals people turn to in order to see the light of faith shed on everyday life. We are trained to bring a theological understanding to human experience. No one else in church or society is trained in matters pertaining to the Christian tradition so as to see the world through the lenses of the gospels. The theological reflection we are called to provide the community holds in dialectical tension the relation of faith and experience in order to make faith-sense of experience and experience-sense of faith. As individuals and as communities, people face hopes (childbirth), fears (death, church closures), life changes (marriage, retirement), moral dilemmas (labor strikes, appropriate care of the dying, where to invest money), tragedies (unemployment, accidental death), and disasters (earthquakes, floods, airplane crashes, war) that call for interpretation and that challenge us with questions of meaning. The way faithful people understand and respond to such experiences can and ought to be informed by their Christian beliefs.

It is one thing to have right knowledge about the Christian tradition and its theological concepts (God, grace, sin, salvation, etc.), but it is a special skill to use this knowledge to help people find meaning and value in their experiences from the perspective of faith. Incarnational theology affirms that "earth is crammed with heaven" so that every experience, if given a chance, can speak to us of God. In the ministries of preaching and teaching, we are like poets or interpreters of obscure texts. By using the stories, images, and symbols of our religious tradition, we try to name grace. To put a finer point on it, in a culture that seems blind to the presence of the divine, we try to help others see life as touched by God and to notice what needs specific attention as a Christian believer. In short, we help believers understand and respond to what is happening in their lives from the perspective of faith and so reclaim, preserve, and strengthen their identity in Christ.

Without theological reflection, the community's commitment of faith can get so far removed from human experience that faith itself becomes irrelevant. But to provide theological reflection for the community requires that we have knowledge and skill for discerning the presence and action of God. This does not mean that everyone in pastoral ministry must become an accomplished academic theologian. But it does mean that, in the midst of the many functions that we are to perform, we ought to have only one focus, God's Word in Jesus Christ, and we ought to serve primarily one purpose, to bring the Word of God to bear on concrete situations in the life of those we serve. This focus and this purpose are what we profess to be able to offer as a theological resource to the community of faith. Such a ministry requires wisdom.

From the perspective of the virtue of wisdom, maintaining our theological competence by developing the habits of reading, study, ongoing education, reflection, and integration is more than a moral requirement. It is a spiritual discipline as well. Acquiring wisdom by maintaining our competence ought to be an integral part of our spiritual life. It is our way of responding to the call and gifts that God has given us for ministry. The time and effort that we put into initial training, ongoing formation, and continuing education through study leaves and sabbaticals can be likened to a form of prayer that binds us to God and to the community we are called to serve.

Some practices to nurture wisdom:

- establishing a regular rhythm for reading and reflection;
- subscribing to a journal in an area of special interest;
- signing up with several publishing houses and keep abreast of new releases;
- taking at least one study week a year and periodic sabbatical;
- joining a reading group;
- taking an occasional course at a nearby college.

## Prudence

If wisdom is the virtue that strives to discover what is true and good for its own sake, then the virtue of prudence is wisdom seeking what is true and good for the sake of action. That is why we often speak of prudence as "practical wisdom," or the application of the wisdom we already possess. What good is it to discover truth and goodness in general if we don't know how to live? We live in the world of particular situations, not in the world of abstract generalizations. While prudence is related to universal truth, its main focus is on individual situations in which action takes place. Prudence is wisdom in action serving the fundamental rule of ethics—do good and avoid evil. With its focus on action, prudence links the intellectual life of wisdom with the moral life of practical behavior.[5]

We need prudence in order to express any of the virtues. All our acquired virtues pass through the portal of prudence to see the light of day. No wonder the ancients knew prudence as the executive virtue, since the others are executed through it. Without prudence we would not know how to be faithful, or how to keep self-care from becoming selfishness, or how to work for justice. Prudence discerns the mean of the virtues by balancing diverse considerations in order to determine the best course of action for now, all things considered. As Aristotle warned when making moral judgments, we should not, however, expect any more precision in our judgments than the nature of our subject matter allows.[6] Prudential reasoning gives us legitimate warrants, or moral certainty, to act in the face of unavoidable uncertainties. But a prudential judgment does not come with mathematical clarity or scientific certainty.

Prudence realizes that we are always taking a risk when deciding what to do. We should not be surprised if conscientious ministers reach differences of opinion on truly ambiguous cases. The best we can do in the face of pastoral urgency is appraise our situations with the highest degree of moral perception we can bring to it. But our judgments will always be contingent, made on the basis of the given facts and our capacities of moral observations. Thus they bear all the marks of fallibility and revisability that belong to practical judgments. Pastoral prudence seeks to avoid, on one extreme, the paralysis of needing absolute certitude before acting and, on the other, the error of premature action. But too many people miss these aspects of prudence because they often mistake it for its false forms, such as timidity (no guts), restraint, expedience, or a calculated self-protectiveness that gets translated as "be careful." But prudence is the decision to act virtuously in the best way possible despite the persistent uncertainty of the outcome.

Prudence in this robust sense is especially necessary today given the trend to develop codes of ethics for pastoral ministers. Much good can come from such projects, such as making explicit the obligations that mark the professional responsibilities of ministry and providing a set of standards to measure responsible pastoral practice and to hold us accountable. There is, however, the serious limitation of expecting rules to make us moral and to make decisions for us. We do not become prudent by memorizing rules, yet it is true that a prudent person knows what the rules are. A code of ethics would be a start, but not the end. While rules are reliable prescriptions for what to do in the normal course of events, rules will not solve the problem of discerning how to respond appropriately in ambiguous situations. Pastoral ministry is filled with an endless variety of pastoral situations, and within those, there is unbounded ambiguity requiring nuance that makes it impossible to predict in advance the best thing to do. The rules of a code of ethics are unable to foresee everything in advance and predict proper behavior. In a famous passage, St. Thomas taught that the more we get into the particulars of a situation, the harder it is for a rule to tell us what to do.[7] We must be able to grasp what is special about a situation and then determine the means that will be good in that context. Ministers who are equipped with prudence will be able to find a way to embody love in the unforeseeable situations of ministry.

Making the right decision is harder than we might think. Pastoral ministers who have struggled with negotiating dual relationships without creating conflicts of interest, or who have tried to preach on a pressing social issue without taking a political side, or who have deliberated on whether and how to speak truth to power know the challenge. Some like to reduce decision making to a "steps-to-follow" decision-tree or to a mathematical-like formula of deduction from principles that guarantee our actions will be right. While a strategy for decision making can guide us and moral principles can inform us, neither can ever tell us precisely the best way to be virtuous in a situation that has so many variables affecting the meaning of our actions. Every moral choice requires some prudential assessment of competing values, principles, and virtues. Prudence must perceive the morally relevant features in play and determine which values and virtues must be expressed to best fit the person who is acting and the context calling for action. In the end, prudence does not guarantee certainty, but it does enable us to assess the complexities as accurately as possible and to approximate as closely as circumstances permit what form goodness should take in a given context.

Prudence also reminds us that having a good intention to do what is right is not enough. For example, we might intend to do what is good for another, but we still must know how to make good on our desires. For example, the parish finance committee wants to contribute to relief efforts after Hurricane Katrina—a good intention for sure. But they still need to decide which person or agency will best make good on their intention. Not all relief services are the same. Even our best intentions must work through prudence to determine the means that will make goodness concrete in this particular situation. Here is where prudence couples with discernment to read the situation and to glean from all its aspects exactly how best to achieve the good. Determining what is right is as much an art as a science. It requires the integration of lessons from experience, keen perception informed by faith, a creative imagination, the foresight of consequences, and the careful deliberation of general rules, immediate facts, and realistic possibilities. The skill of bringing all of this together in the most fitting way possible is the function of prudence.

In a morally complex world, our decisions will ultimately emerge from the quality of our prudence. Thomas Aquinas gave perhaps the best description of the parts of prudence.[8] I need only to summarize his vision here to show what a robust understanding of prudence requires.

Prudence uses memory. Rather than relying only on universal rules for guidance, prudence learns from experience. It remembers past experiences, our own and others', to see if there is anything similar in the past that can serve as a guide in determining what to do in this new experience. While experience is important for prudence to function well, not just any experience will do. Experiences are a dime a dozen. Rarer is reflected experience from which we have learned a lesson and so accumulated moral wisdom. This accumulated wisdom becomes a source of information about right and wrong. We all probably know people who have been in ministry for ten years or more but really have only one year's experience because so little reflection has gone on. We could not expect them to have the quality of perception or the accumulated moral wisdom needed for good decision making even though they have been in ministry for a number of years. Similarly, as Aristotle pointed out, we do not expect to find much prudence in young people or even in those who are "young" at a new role, like being a minister.[9] The "young" do not yet have enough experience relative to their role in ministry to learn by comparison or to draw analogies. If we have not yet acquired wisdom from reflecting on experience, then we would do well to follow the guidance of rules and the supervision of those in authority who have more wisdom.

Prudence also requires insight. We cannot deliberate accurately about what to do until we can "see into" the particulars of the situation. From there we must distinguish the morally relevant features from the peripheral, know which principles apply, and look into the future to anticipate what values will be protected and what will be lost in the consequences of our actions.

Prudence is teachable, for it values the skills of seeking and accepting guidance. Here prudence partners with humility and wisdom to admit that we don't know everything. If having a true sense of things is necessary to act rightly, and if we know that we don't know all that we need to know about the situation and can't get all the information we need on our own, then we should be willing to seek counsel from others, especially those whose experience gives them a greater vantage point to see what we might miss. Prudence taps the wisdom of those with broader experience who have lived through similar situations. Thus the important role of supervision and mentoring programs in ministry and of moral authorities in the decision-making process.

Prudence also reasons well about what moves to make. Reasoning well means that we take into account everything that is pertinent to the situation. We keep asking questions, especially "What am I missing?" until we have uncovered all the relevant factors and imagined a host of possibilities, difficulties, and outcomes that could ensue from trading off the values at stake. This reasoning is so demanding that it begs us to consult with others in the process. In addition, it ought to be done in a prayerful manner so as to be open to the Holy Spirit. The Spirit can guide us as we sift through factors and options, strain to catch subtleties in circumstances and notice how we are drawn to act. In this way, prudence is closely aligned with the virtue of discernment.

Prudence pays attention to circumstances. Circumstances are important because an action that is fitting in one context (holding on your lap the six-year-old neighbor girl while at the neighborhood picnic) may, despite good intentions, be wrong in another (holding a six-year-old girl on your lap while alone in your office to explain the First Communion program). This simple example illustrates why doing what is right requires that we know the circumstances and spot whatever might have an impact on the meaning of our actions.

According to St. Thomas, "actions are good or bad according to the circumstances."[10] Our intention exists in relational tension with the means and all the aspects that make up the circumstances. Only by considering the action in the context of its qualifying circumstances can we determine the true moral meaning of the action. We can uncover the relevant circumstances by asking reality-revealing questions: Who is involved? What is going on? When and where is it happening? Why is it being done? and How is it being done?[11] In order for prudence to balance means to ends, prudence needs to grasp all these features that make any specific situation unique.

Closely related to circumspection is foresight. Prudence looks ahead, not just to near-term but also to long-term consequences, to see what might follow. This requires imagination sufficient to estimate, anticipate, and even live in a future when the outcome of our actions will have produced either good or harm. What might work in the short term (if I work later into the night I will get this project done on time) can have negative effects in the long term (I will not be very alert at tomorrow's meeting when it gets discussed). Withholding my opinion at the meeting may keep me from being criticized in the short run but it can undermine the dynamics of cooperation in the long run.

Shortsightedness makes caution a necessary component of prudence. Caution can easily be mistaken for the whole of the virtue of prudence and reduce a robust virtue to timidity. But caution means that prudence is reluctant to shoot from the hip. It wants to take aim and give the decision-making process time. So it moves slowly in order to guard against a hasty decision that would cause harm—harm that could have been avoided or lessened if we had paid attention to more factors and considered more fully the circumstances and consequences. Too often we cause harm not because we are mean-spirited but because we are simply careless. Our moral choices come with a mix of aspects, some of which help and some of which hinder the well-being of persons and the environment. We do not live in a world where good is purely good and evil is just plain evil. Good and evil are entangled like the weeds and the wheat of Jesus' parable (Matt 13:24-30, 36b-42). As the story reminds us, good and evil can be so intertwined as to be indistinguishable. None of us enjoys such sharp moral vision or such unsullied clarity that we can make a clear-cut distinction between them. Caution gives us time to distinguish and separate them as best we can. If we go slow and give ourselves time, we may better separate the good from the bad so that what we finally do will make life good in fact and not just in appearance. In order to honor this requirement of time and prudence as a process, we need to avoid the habit of filling up every moment of the day with activity. We ought to create a rhythm of making quiet space for reflection. Here is where prudence couples with discernment and our spiritual disciplines of creating space for quiet and for opening ourselves to the Holy Spirit.

But when there is little or no time to think thoroughly about what to do, we must rely on the acumen that comes from having practiced prudence when we had the chance. Practicing prudent decision making habitually can give us an uncanny ability to do what is right even when we can't slow ourselves down to think about it as much as we would like. We have probably met this ability in some of the more seasoned ministers whom we admire. How did they know so quickly the right thing to do when a colleague begins to disrupt the committee's process? They know from the practice of judging wisely when they had the chance. As with all the virtues, we learn prudence through practice. Only gradually are we able to deal with situations and make decisions in the way a wise person does.

While prudence is the virtue that gives us the skill to focus on the right means for achieving the good now, it is also the virtue that enables ministers to connect what we do now with the larger mission of making the reign of God visible. Prudence presumes a vision of the good life toward which we are always striving and against which we measure our progress. What we determine to be prudent, or the form we believe goodness should take, depends in the end on our vision of what life is all about. Moral disagreements reflect the reality that we do not all share the same view of what constitutes the good life.

What we determine to be a good life ought to be informed by our Christian beliefs. Jesus gave us his vision of the good life in the symbol of the reign of God. Under God's reign, love rules. The good life is to love God and to love our neighbor as we love ourselves. In

Jesus' vision of life ruled by love, we ought to strive to live in harmony and peace with everyone and with the earth. He showed the way. We are to follow by imitating his freedom and faithfulness today. The paragons of prudence today are those who are able to live this dream of God and make it visible by showing mercy, seeking justice, and working for peace.

Some practices that cultivate and express prudence are:

- taking time to be silent and still;
- fostering the discipline of self-reflection;
- knowing our Achilles heels in decision making to make sure they don't foreshorten the process;
- holding back from snap decisions for what else might be waiting to be noticed;
- paying attention to details and discriminating among their degrees of importance;
- trusting ourselves in our diligence and in our sense of how-much-time-is-enough when it comes to making a decision;
- recognizing that we have in fact made wise decisions;
- consulting with an openness to learn from the experience of others;
- working with a mentor, spiritual director, counselor, or friend who can keep us honest with ourselves;
- coming to a decision in a timely manner.

As the communities we serve become more and more well educated not only in secular matters but also in religious ones, we will need to maintain a like competence if we are to serve them effectively. The drive of wisdom to grasp what is true and of prudence to judge rightly about what actions to take are virtues that cannot be minimized in any ministry that is to advance the mission of the church. Without a desire for wisdom and the habit of thinking through actions to take our people will perish.

# 5

## Developing Pastorally

The pastoral ministry is how the church makes present God's saving care for all peoples. In this way, ministry is a function of the mission of the church—to be both a sign and an instrument of our union with God and of the unity of all humankind (LG 1). To accomplish this mission, we need to develop pastorally by acquiring virtues that soften our individuality and build up our relationships with others. Four virtues serve this end: justice, compassion, generosity, and courage.

### Justice

If the mission of the church defines the goal of pastoral ministry, then justice is the virtue that aims our ministry toward that end. In the first chapter, I referred to James Keenan's relational model of the virtues. He posits justice as the cardinal virtue that governs our general relationships. I could have included justice under the virtues for developing humanly as a relational being. It fits very well there. I have moved it to the pastoral dimension, however, to show not only that developing pastorally interfaces with developing humanly but also to underscore that ministry happens in relationships. Justice is the elementary moral disposition for getting along with one another. It governs the ties that bind us to each other, to God, and to all of creation.

"That's not fair" expresses a child's earliest moral insight about the way relationships ought to work. Justice comes to grips with the fact that fairness does not flourish. Justice recognizes that there are selves other than ourselves, that they too are valuable, and that we need to take them seriously. Without justice, we could not get along. We would be like black holes in space sucking everything into ourselves. But justice chastens our egoism and breaks us out of our self-centered isolation. Justice draws our attention to others so that we will live with others in mind. In his *A New American Justice*, Daniel Maguire puts it well: "Justice is the first assault upon egoism. Egoism would say: 'To me my own.' Justice says, 'Wait. There are other *selves*.' Personal existence is a shared glory."[1] He succinctly calls justice "the cornerstone of human togetherness."[2]

The virtue of justice extends its tendrils deep into the soil of an anthropology of relatedness. As we saw in chapter 1, we flourish humanly through respectful interrelationships. Such a view is in line with the dominant perspective of modern science that understands the whole of the created world to be basically a field of ongoing interactions and interrelations. Justice relies on the fact that human life is a shared life. We are inextricably enmeshed with others in a web of relationships that are constitutive of our identity. To give others their due is to recognize how much they are a part of us. A metal placard at a trailhead in Yosemite National Park has a quote from John Muir that could very well serve as a one-sentence argument for why we need justice: "When we try to pick out something by itself, we find it hitched to everything else in the universe." Justice is the virtue that pulls us away from the temptation to plot out our lives without taking into account the impact our behavior might have on others. Justice habitually disposes us to see our needs and interests as inseparable from the needs and interests of others.

The biblical view of justice is rooted in the covenant that forms one people bonded to one another and to God. The insight of the covenant is that we are not a loose association of individuals standing side by side and held together by self-interest. We are an interdependent community where individual good is bound up with the good of the whole. This covenantal, relational understanding of the self has wide-ranging implications for understanding justice and for the importance of sustaining right relationships with others, with God, and with all creation.

In the Bible, when justice is ignored, the prophets cry out that the covenant is broken. Something is wrong in the relation between society and its members, and in their relation to God. Such a view stands in stark contrast to our usual American way of understanding justice. In Washington DC stands the symbol of American justice—a blindfolded woman holding balanced scales. Notice the imagery. Balanced scales suggest arithmetic equality. The blindness suggests that the judicial decision is not concerned with the person affected by the judgment but only with the reality being judged. American justice focuses on fairness in procedures and equality in outcomes irrespective of the person. When we put this image of justice as impartial and equal alongside the Bible, we can only be struck by the illogic of God.

Picture a loaf of bread in the middle of a table. Around the table are people of different ages, ethnic backgrounds, nations, abilities, and socio-economic status. The bread is to be divided among them. What is the most just way to do this? The American sense of justice would say that the loaf of bread should be divided equally. It is blind to the larger duty we have to the common good and to the social ties that bind us to one another, especially to the weakest among us. The biblical sense of justice, by contrast, takes the blindfold off. It knows that the scales don't balance. Instead of scales and an impartial blindfold, biblical justice would find out who is most in need and then would divide the loaf to aid the neediest. According to biblical justice, need, not merit or fair procedures, is the basic criterion for distributing resources.

Two of the strongest prophetic texts affirming that faith involves doing justice are from Jeremiah and Isaiah. In Jeremiah we read:

Thus says the LORD: Act with justice and righteousness, and deliver from the hand of the oppressor anyone who has been robbed. And do no wrong or violence to the alien, the orphan, and the widow, or shed innocent blood in this place. . . .

> Are you a king
>> because you compete in cedar?
> Did not your father eat and drink
>> and do justice and righteousness?
>> Then it was well with him.
> He judged the cause of the poor and needy;
>> then it was well.
> Is not this to know me?
>> says the LORD. (Jer 22:3, 15-16)

From Isaiah, we read,

> Is such the fast that I choose,
>> a day to humble oneself?
> Is it to bow down the head like a bulrush,
>> and to lie in sackcloth and ashes?
> Will you call this a fast,
>> a day acceptable to the LORD?
> Is not this the fast that I choose:
>> to loose the bonds of injustice,
>> to undo the thongs of the yoke,
> to let the oppressed go free,
>> and to break every yoke?
> Is it not to share your bread with the hungry,
>> and bring the homeless poor into your house;
> when you see the naked, to cover them,
>> and not to hide yourself from your own kin?
> Then your light shall break forth like the dawn,
>> and your healing shall spring up quickly;
> your vindicator shall go before you,
>> the glory of the LORD shall be your rear guard.
> Then you shall call, and the LORD will answer;
>> you shall cry for help, and he will say, Here I am.
>> (Isa 58:5-9)

In these texts, true religion—knowing God and praising God in religious ritual—is equated with taking up the causes of the poor and the needy. These two texts, along with the following from Amos, strongly indict religious practices in the absence of the work of justice as empty devotions that are repugnant to God.

> I hate, I despise your festivals,
>> and I take no delight in your solemn assemblies.
> Even though you offer me your burnt offerings and grain
>> offerings,
>> I will not accept them;
> and the offerings of well-being of your fatted animals
>> I will not look upon.
> Take away from me the noise of your songs;
>> I will not listen to the melody of your harps.
> But let justice roll down like waters,
>> and righteousness like an ever-flowing stream.
> (Amos 5:21-24)

The imagery is striking. By comparing justice to rushing water, Amos shows that without justice there can be no life in the land.

In the tradition of the prophets, Jesus revealed God's love for "the lost, the least, and the last" over and over again. Jesus reached out to women and to those considered outcasts. He took up the cause of those who suffered religious and social discrimination. He crossed the line between Jews and Samaritans. He reached out to Gentiles, welcomed children. He showed mercy to sinners. His ministry not only engaged the outcasts, but it also reintegrated them into the community. For example, he declares that Zacchaeus "too is a son of Abraham" (Luke 19:9) and so recognized him as a rightful member of the community. Similarly, Jesus addresses the bent over woman as "a daughter of Abraham" (Luke 13:16) to facilitate her reentry into the community after her healing. Luke's Jesus echoes Isaiah to say something about how we are to live together when he proclaims in his inaugural sermon, "The Spirit of the Lord is upon me, because he has anointed me to bring good news to the poor. He has sent me to proclaim release to the captives and recovery of sight to the blind, to let the oppressed go free, to proclaim the year of the Lord's favor" (Luke 4:18-19). Matthew's Jesus makes clear not only that we are to care for the poor but also that we are to be identified with the poor as Jesus is. The last judgment scene in the parable of the Sheep and the Goats tells us that Jesus, who came as Emmanuel (God with us), so identifies with the poor as to lie hidden in our midst, wrapping himself in those most in need— the hungry, the naked, the homeless, the sick, and the imprisoned. What we do to these, we do to Jesus (Matt 25:31-46). In effect, the parable says that our judgment lies in how we stand with the poor and do corporal works of mercy for those in need. To reject the poor is to reject God manifest in them.

From these biblical roots, our understanding of justice has continued to evolve and grow through the Christian tradition. Three of its themes help us understand the roots and reach of the virtue of justice for pastoral ministry—that we are sacred, committed to the common good, and give a preferential option for the poor.

First, the roots of justice lie in the very reason that we would want to take others seriously in the first place. Justice says that everyone deserves his or her due because everyone matters. To deny justice to another is to declare him or her worthless. The virtuous disposition of justice grows out of the rich soil of our conviction that the inalienable dignity or basic worth of each person is rooted in being made in the image of God. Our dignity does not depend on race, sex, economic status, social contribution, or personal achievements. We share a fundamental equality before God by virtue of our inherent dignity. We would not feel indebted to another, or be disposed to take the well-being of others into account, if we did not believe in our fundamental equality or saw no value in each other. Paul Wadell puts it well when he writes, "Injustice is possible, indeed inevitable, as long as we convince ourselves that all human beings are not equal in the eyes of God and that not all human beings have value and worth and dignity."[3] But because we take seriously that people are of value and radically equal before God, justice disposes us in ministry to promote the well-being of all and to protest attempts to sacrifice anyone's dignity for the enhancement of a few.

Second, the human person is not only sacred but also social. Human life is a shared life. Justice reminds us that we are not the center of the universe. There are other centers of life and we are to give proper weight to their claims on us. With justice we know that cooperation is better than playing Lone Ranger, and that give-and-take is better than grab-and-go. We are better together than we are alone; and we flourish through respectful interrelationship. The reach of justice is that everyone should share in the basic goods necessary for participating in the human community. We call this working for the common good.[4]

The common good is not the sum total of individual goods, nor is it the good of the majority trumping the good of the rest. While it respects and serves the interests of individual persons, the common good ultimately upholds the good of society as a whole to be more important than the good of any one individual. The common good believes that the individual will flourish only insofar as society as a whole flourishes. A commitment to the common good forces us to recognize that, while there are some things that we must want for ourselves or our favorite sectors of the church community (such as our youth group or our liturgy committee), we might not pursue them right now so that the good of the whole might be better served. Justice reminds us that the needs and interests of others are really inseparable from our own and that our own flourishing as individuals is tied to how well others fare. In short, the common good keeps the best interests of the individual and the well-being of the community as a whole in tension. Its achievement depends on the generosity and commitment of individuals and institutions to seek those actions and policies that will provide for the good of the individual as well as for the good of others.

Third, the biblical test of the reach of justice is our treatment of the poor. But who are the poor? They are those whose dignity is on the line. We readily recognize them on the street or in the evening news as the ones lacking material goods of food, clothing, and shelter. But the poor are also those who have no voice to advocate on their own and so are powerless to influence public policies. One of the striking features of the Lukan parable of the Rich Man and Lazarus (Luke 16:19-31) is that the rich man has no name, but he does have a strong voice to advocate his cause. Lazarus, by contrast, has a name by which he can be identified, but he has no voice by which to be heard. Justice is committed to seeing that the poor have basic material resources as well as a voice so that they can defend themselves and not be excluded from social life, the marketplace, or the workforce.

Why are we to stand with the poor? Very simply, because God does. As partners in the covenant, we are to value what God values. Human justice is to reflect divine justice. When God took the side of the oppressed Hebrew slaves in Egypt, delivered them to safety, and pitched tent among them, God was showing that their suffering and hopes were God's very own. The prophets frequently had to remind the chosen people that the quality of their faith depended on the character of their justice. This was tested by how they treated the oppressed and the outsiders—"the widow, the orphan, and the stranger." Justice joins with hospitality to expand the circle of those whose needs become our concern. Injustice ignores them and does not worry about whether they are getting their due.

We are able to give a preferential option for the poor when justice partners with solidarity. In the opening sentence of one of the major documents of the Second Vatican Council, *Gaudium et Spes* (The Church in the Modern World), the church expressed in an unprecedented way its solidarity with the entire human family: "The joys and the hopes, the griefs and the anxieties of men and women of this age, especially of those who are poor or in any way afflicted, these too are the joys and hopes, the griefs and anxieties of the followers of Christ" (GS 1). In this document, the church defined itself as a church-for-others. Its task is to bear the burden with other people, to struggle with others for justice, and to strengthen the bonds that unite people despite their differences. So when it comes to standing with the poor in solidarity, our voice cannot be mute and we cannot check our faith at the door when we meet to examine our economic, social, and political structures.

Pope John Paul II spoke of solidarity as a virtue in his social encyclical, *Sollicitudo Rei Socialis* (December 30, 1987): "[Solidarity] then is not a feeling of vague compassion or shallow distress at the misfortunes of so many people, both near and far. On the contrary, it is a firm and persevering determination to commit oneself to the common good; that is to say to the good of all and of each individual because we are all really responsible for all" (38). Solidarity is not fully realized until we live out our commitment to justice by becoming responsible to and for one another.

Nurturing justice can occur in three movements—seeing, judging, and acting.[5] First, we must begin to *see differently*. Paul Wadell captures this well with his notion of the compassionate imagination as the prerequisite for justice. His point is that, while it is true that we act according to how we see, our vision can be so distorted that we miss what is right before our eyes, "especially," he insists, "if what we might see would challenge us to change."[6] For example, patriarchal societies can skew men's vision so that they do not see women as their equals; many heterosexuals suffer the myopia that distorts their vision of gays and lesbians as truly their equals in God. Injustice grows from distorted vision. A compassionate imagination allows us to project ourselves into another's situation and perceive their plight more vividly. It is harder to neglect what we can feel and experience for ourselves. Refusing to risk imagining another's predicament allows us to remain complacent and our behavior remains unchanged.

While it is always right to begin by meeting our responsibilities to those nearest us, our vision must grow to become more global. An ancient rabbi had a saying that gives us an image for the person of expansive vision and interest. "He who cares for his own child is like a stream which nourishes a tree along its banks. But he who loves another's child is like a cloud which goes from the sea into the desert and waters there a lonesome tree." When God inquired after the missing Abel, Cain gave the surly response, "Am I my brother's keeper?" (Gen 4:9). Cain's question makes us think of our refusal to see beyond our inner circle to include society's weakest members—children, the elderly, immigrants—and so to be indifferent toward relations between peoples even when basic values such as survival, freedom, or peace are at stake. But we can no longer limit our vision or our caring to those in our own family. We must include the whole human family and the earth. We are all our "brother's keeper" for God has entrusted each of us to one another.

Living in the global village as we do makes it imperative that we see everyone as sharing in fundamental equality and dignity. An ancient rabbi asked his students how they could tell when night had ended and day was on its way back. "Could it be when you see an animal in the distance and can tell whether it is a sheep or a dog?" "No," answered the rabbi. "Could it be when you look at a tree in the distance and can tell whether it is a fig tree or a peach tree?" "No." "Well, then," the students demanded, "when is it?" "It is when you look on the face of any man or woman and see that she or he is your brother or sister. Because if you cannot do that, then no matter what time it is, it is still night."[7] To look into the face of any other and to see a sister or brother is seeing with a compassionate imagination. When we can project ourselves into the experience of the poor and know them as people whose lives are filled with joy and sorrow, love and hope, success and failure like our own, then we are less likely to tolerate racial, ethnic, political, or sexist discrimination against them.

Second, once we begin to see differently, we must begin to *judge differently*. Our lives extend beyond a private relationship with God and our neighbor to participate in the whole social order—local practices, social structures, institutional policies. Developing a compassionate imagination can open us to a "structural vision" that sees beyond individual human need to the structures that must be changed if the human need is ever to be addressed judiciously. Any practice, structure, or policy is inherently unjust which takes difference (of gender, race, social status, or education) to mean someone is inferior and so can be excluded or exploited. Our lives are inevitably marked by the structural relationships that can act for or against an individual's rights and the common good. Injustice inevitably flowers when it becomes the logical consequence of structures based on the superiority of some and the inferiority of all the rest, and when it allows those who claim superiority to dominate in the name of service.

Our decision making today must include a range of implications much wider than our own immediate interest. In terms of global structures and interests—communication, transportation, economics, politics, and the environment—we are more connected than ever before. For example, we are quite familiar today with how our domestic economic issues impinge on foreign markets, how environmental carelessness in one region affects ecosystems far beyond it. Our interconnectedness in the choices we make and in the deeds we do is clearly visible in this humorous but pointed story. Three men go rowing together in one boat. One begins to drill a hole in the boat underneath his seat. The other two panic and scream to him in their fear, "What do you think you're doing?" With calm detachment, he answers, "What is it to you? I am only making the hole under my own seat."

When making plans or setting up a new social or economic structure, an important question to ask from the perspective of justice and solidarity is the following: "How will this impact the poor and disadvantaged?" From this perspective, the U.S. bishops, in their pastoral letter Economic Justice for All (1986), say that we ought to keep three concerns before us when making plans and distributing resources: "Decisions must be judged in light of what they do *for* the poor, what they do *to* the poor, and what they enable the poor to do *for themselves*" (24). Judging proposals in light of these concerns challenges us not to take for granted the way things are but to look with critical suspicion at how decisions and structures serve all people, but especially the poor.

The third movement in nurturing justice is to *act differently*. In the face of so much need, we ask "What can I do?" In terms of justice, acting differently is a matter of overcoming narcissism. What can we do to challenge the self-serving ways we see the world? How can we contribute to creating a just social order? More often than not, we feel powerless before the enormity of poverty and the extent of misery. So we ought to begin small by raising our consciousness about the direction our lives are taking and the situations in society that we help to create and sustain. Then we can start sowing seeds of justice.

One place to begin is with our most common spiritual practice, the Eucharist. When we gather to give thanks and praise to God, we also commit ourselves to care about what God cares about. Paying attention to the stories of Scripture, the liturgical prayers, and the ritual actions of the community informs our imaginations to see from the point of view of God. The vision and values reflected in the Eucharist call us to build an inclusive social order. We who have been reconciled to God and to one another around the table are to be instruments of reconciliation with those who are marginalized. Participating in the Eucharist can and ought to foster a sense of solidarity with those with whom we worship and for whom we pray. The Eucharist can tutor us in solidarity by providing experiences where bonds of affection with others have a chance to grow. My own parish, Holy Spirit/Newman Hall at the University of California in Berkeley, reminds us that the Eucharist is about receiving, giving, and sharing by sponsoring a JustFaith program of study, prayer, and social involvement, by hosting a monthly meal for the homeless, and by announcing each week the social agency that will receive five percent of the week's collection. These are ways to acquire a vision of the interconnectedness of all humanity, to foster solidarity with the poor, and to expand the horizon of our world beyond self-interest.

Another way to raise our consciousness regarding our social reality is to welcome into our lives people different from ourselves. Justice grows when we practice hospitality to strangers—people who do not share our assumptions about life, people of different political persuasions, people of different racial and ethnic backgrounds, people with different gender and sexual orientations, people from different faith traditions or religions. By being hospitable to difference, we can become aware of our own prejudices and perhaps discover that many of our esteemed attitudes and honored practices are really unjust. Justice must join with humility if we are to be open enough to be influenced by difference. Otherwise, we will only continue to assess everything in terms of what we call good.

We can sow seeds of justice through education. Justice requires that we take time to become informed about the society in which we live, its institutions, policies, and practices. We especially need to pay attention to voices from the margin in order to learn from a perspective we too easily ignore. Forging ties with the marginalized will allow the poor to teach us. Our education should also include hands-on service learning followed by developing our skills of social analysis to understand the dynamics of human interdependence and to identify the structures marked by sin. We need to know the impact these structures have especially on those who lack access to power in society or the church if we are to contribute toward facilitating reform.

We act justly, too, when we provide the service we say we can provide by virtue of our role. If our ministry is just, we will not take advantage of our role and its power by giving priority to satisfying our own needs and interests. We will, rather, give due deference to the needs of those we are called to serve. Accountability is also a way of doing justice to the community. We act justly when we observe standards of professional conduct and the criteria for fairness in employment practices, such as in procedures for hiring and firing and for fair compensation. We also act justly when we oppose any financial arrangements that mismanage funds or curry favor through financial privileges. Justice is at work when we look at those who are at the table and ask, "Who's missing?" Justice wants to be inclusive in offering service so that whole groups of people do not get neglected or marginalized from our spiritual care, such as the youth, the singles, the elderly, the shut-ins, the gay and lesbian community, and so forth. Moreover, a just ministry cooperates with social and ecclesial policies that promote collaboration among the churches and social agencies to share resources, such as shelters for the homeless, food banks, and treatment and prevention programs for those with HIV/AIDS.

A just ministry also opposes any structures and practices in which people are victimized sexually through harassment or abuse. Acting justly can begin with using inclusive language and resisting racist or sexist slurs and maintaining appropriate boundaries in our professional relationships. We can also act justly by monitoring our own purchasing practices and investments to see whether we are supporting corporations that have policies that advance the cause of the poor. Justice couples with generosity when we are mindful of our overall consumption of goods and the accumulation of possessions. Small steps such as these may not effect great change in the world, but they can have a great effect on us. In the life of virtue, who we are deep down spills over into our lives. What we do, over time, makes us who we are.

Living by the virtue of justice is hardly easy, yet none of us can do pastoral ministry without being just. Justice is essential to the proclamation of the Gospel.[8] According to Johann Baptist Metz, conversion to justice demands rejecting an "anthropology of domination" by which we define ourselves over and against others and allow domination "to become the secret regulating principle of all interpersonal relationships."[9] With justice, no one is dominated; everyone is served. Injustice works otherwise. To live justly, Metz suggests we learn to practice nondominating human virtues, like gratitude and humility, which we explored in chapter 2, and compassion and generosity, which we will examine next.

Some practices that cultivate and express justice are:

- welcoming into our lives people different from ourselves;
- using inclusive language and acting inclusively in providing service;
- keeping informed about major social issues of the day;
- attending to issues of justice among employees of our parish and schools;
- collaborating with community agencies on projects of mutual concern;
- serving each person and sector of the parish without discrimination;
- encouraging a preferential option for the poor;
- promoting a sustainable environment.

### Compassion

Like justice, compassion expands the horizon of our world and reminds us that a morally integrated spirituality must be relational. But whereas justice is the virtue directed toward our general relationships, social transformation, and the common good, compassion is the virtue that attends to the suffering of particular persons with whom we have direct contact. In my informal surveys at workshops on professional ethics in ministry, compassion appears universally on the list of virtues necessary for ministry. My conclusion is that the vast majority of ministers regard some notion of fellow-feeling as the signature feature of pastoral ministry. Should this surprise us? Not really. The Christian moral tradition has so associated compassion with the central quality of God and of Jesus that we can reasonably expect that a religious person would seek to embody it. Without compassion, ministry would collapse into a self-interested concern for one's own salvation.

Compassion has its roots in the very character of God and God's saving action toward us in Jesus. The compassion of God is Jesus' willingness to empty himself, become human, and take on the role of the suffering servant all the way through death and resurrection in order to reconcile us to God and to one another. Jesus did not sit on the sidelines as a detached observer of human suffering. He disclosed the character of God's love by joining in solidarity with those who suffer. When Jesus exhorted us to be compassionate as God is compassionate (Luke 6:36), he underscored compassion as inseparable from holiness, from being like God in whose image we are made.

In speaking about God in maternal metaphors, Elizabeth Johnson further illuminates divine compassion by comparing it to a mother's concern for her children. God as mother is concerned not only with the good of a privileged few but with the well-being of the entire world, and so her attention is turned toward those most in need. For Johnson, the compassionate God, spoken about in analogy with women's experience of relationality and care, can awaken in us responsible action in the face of suffering.[10]

Jesus modeled compassion both by his inclusivity with his reaching out to those in distress regardless of their class, gender, or moral state, and by his hands-on help offering relief (Matt 9:36; 14:14; 15:32; 20:34; Mark 1:40-44; 6:34; 8:2; Luke 7:13). Jesus also exhorted compassion in his teaching through parables. Two stand out: the judgment parable of the Sheep and the Goats (Matt 25:31-46), and the Good Samaritan (Luke 10:25-37). The judgment parable gives us concrete benchmarks for assessing the quality of our spirituality. We have come to know these measures as the corporal works of mercy—feed the hungry, give drink to the thirsty, shelter the homeless, clothe the naked, visit the sick, visit the imprisoned, and bury the dead. The parable is striking in how it makes the practice of compassion the measure of our holiness.

The Good Samaritan is the biblical paragon of compassion. The Samaritan's gut-wrenching feeling for the victim in the ditch motivated him to take steps to see that the victim would be cared for in a healing way. Jesus tells this story in response to the scribe's question, "Who is my neighbor?" The parable shows that my neighbor is not the one in need but the one who shows compassion. That is what neighbors do—they act on behalf of the one suffering. The parable ends with the moral injunction, "Go and do likewise." We are to show neighbor-love by being compassionate whenever we have the chance.

When I have pressed ministerial groups to explain the virtue of compassion, I have found that many use it simply to mean love in general. Taking compassion for love is quite understandable when we consider the rich semantic field that surrounds this virtue. It carries a dizzying array of meanings. Compassion is often understood as virtually synonymous with kindness, benevolence, sympathy, care, empathy, pity, and mercy. It is also the meaning intended by various expressions, such as "being moved with pity," "feeling sorry for," "my heart goes out to," "a gut-wrenching feeling for," or "have sympathy for." Sometimes these terms and expressions are equivalent, but usually there is a difference.

While compassion is indeed an expression of love, it is a special kind of love. Martha Nussbaum's semantic analysis shows that we cannot conflate love with compassion. She carefully teases out the important shades of difference between compassion, empathy, sympathy, and pity. While closely related, they are not the same. The Latin roots of compassion mean "to suffer with." Compassion includes not only a deep feeling for others who are suffering, but also the regret for what is happening and the desire to do something to help. Compassion is not passive. It is not a self-absorbing emotional state. For Nussbaum, the constitutive feature of compassion is that another's suffering so matters to me that I am willing to get personally involved by responding in ways that are helpful in relieving their distress.[11]

Empathy is not quite the same thing. For Nussbaum, empathy is an ability to "feel into" another's experience by reconstructing imaginatively what it might be. With empathy, we mirror the other's experience. I empathize with you before you get up to preach because I know how nervous you must feel. Empathy shares in another's feelings almost as if they were one's own, but it stops short of making any particular evaluation of them.[12] Nor is empathy necessarily doing something. That belongs to compassion. Compassion is empathy linked with judging that the other person's situation is bad and that we would be suffering too in that situation. It moves us out of ourselves to give attention to the other's plight and also entails doing what we can to improve it. Sympathy is akin to compassion in that it includes an evaluation that the other person is distressed. Pity, on the other hand, has a more insulting connotation for Nussbaum. It suggests condescension and superiority over those who suffer. Pity suggests inequality whereas compassion and sympathy make sense among equals.[13]

The following story, "The Old Grandfather and the Grandson," by Leo Tolstoy shows well the close link of empathy and compassion:

> The grandfather had become very old. His legs wouldn't go, his eyes didn't see, his ears didn't hear, he had no teeth. And when he ate, the food dripped from his mouth.
>
> The son and daughter-in-law stopped setting a place for him at the table and gave him supper in back of the stove. Once they brought dinner down to him in a cup. The old man wanted to move the cup and dropped and broke it. The daughter-in-law began to grumble at the old man for spoiling everything in the house and breaking the cups and said that she would now give him dinner in a dishpan. The old man only sighed and said nothing.
>
> Once the husband and wife were staying at home and watching their small son playing on the floor with some wooden planks: he was building something. The father asked: "What is that you are doing, Misha?" And Misha said: "Dear Father, I am making a dishpan. So what when you and dear Mother become old, you may be fed from this dishpan."
>
> The husband and wife looked at one another and began to weep. They became ashamed of so offending the old man, and from then on seated him at the table and waited on him.[14]

This story captures the power of our imaginative ability to close the distance and difference between us by sharing in someone else's feelings and experience as if they were our own. Through empathy we overcome our difference and develop a sense of sameness. We recognize that we are united by the deeper truth of our solidarity in a common humanity. Once we recognize how much we are the same through empathy, then our acts of compassion come from a space of communion.

The distinctive features of compassion—sensing that we would be suffering too in the same or a like situation, reaching out to relieve what we can and to help in bearing what we can't relieve—stand out clearly when seen against their opposite, cruelty. Cruelty is to close oneself off from another's feelings, not to take their suffering seriously, to laugh at it, or to walk away and ignore it. Cruelty even takes advantage of another's misfortune, as the husband and wife did when they set no place for the grandfather at the table but gave him supper in a dishpan in back of the stove. The cruel are not moved by being in communion with a common humanity to do anything that relieves suffering. Torturers, for example, can have the empathy to imagine what their victim is suffering, yet they take delight in it and use it for selfish purposes. While empathy need not necessarily be linked to beneficent action, compassion always is.

Research on the role of empathy as the prerequisite for compassion shows how it is the cornerstone to a moral life.[15] It is the first link in a long chain of moral development, it leads to altruistic behavior, and it is the psychological prerequisite for moral reasoning. Our fundamental moral obligation is to treat others with dignity. The way we get to know others well enough to treat them with dignity is through empathy—to see things and to feel things the way they do. That is why the advice Atticus Finch gives to his daughter, Scout, in *To Kill a Mockingbird* is so apt for establishing a moral outlook on life. After having a tough day at school, where she strained her relationships with her teacher and classmates, Atticus advises, "If you can learn a simple trick, Scout, you'll get along a lot better with all kinds of folks. You never really understand a person until you consider things from his point of view . . . until you climb into his skin and walk around in it."[16] Without the knowledge that comes from empathy, we could not know others in their unique individuality. No wonder empathy is the ethical basis of all helping professions. It is the first step toward acquiring the virtue of compassion.

Unless our feelings are totally numb, we cannot stand to see another suffer. Seeing tears fall from another's eyes causes tears to well up in our own. Empathy is at work here. First we notice people are suffering and then we try to understand their suffering more deeply. Compassion follows when our emotional connection moves us to do what we can to relieve suffering. Feeling another's suffering and acting on that feeling to bring relief is not codependency. Quite the contrary. Codependency is acting on one's own need to be needed regardless of what the other feels or needs.

One of the greatest obstacles to strengthening the habit of compassion is apathy—distancing ourselves from any feelings for another. When we set professional boundaries, we are careful not to get overly involved in the lives of others. So we keep our emotional distance along with our physical distance. Sometimes apathy comes disguised as professionalism. They are not the same. Professional boundaries respect another's feelings and create a safe space for the other to feel the feelings without fear of manipulation. Apathy is what the biblical writers called a "hard heart." That is, we know we can make a difference, but we don't care to. We have no desire to relieve suffering. If we were to harbor such a disposition, ministry would self-destruct. Ministry thrives, however, when we maintain appropriate boundaries. Without empathy and compassion, we would be cold and cruel, hardhearted and indifferent bystanders. Or, we would fall into codependency where we might feel the feelings of others but have no center of our own from which to respond.

Compassion "suffers with" another who is suffering. But suffering with another is hard. We often don't know what to do about another's suffering, how to explain it, or how to make use of it. Suffering, according to Dr. Eric Cassell in his work *The Nature of Suffering,* is a psychological or spiritual state characteristically marked by severe distress or a range of emotions induced by threats to our well-being and the loss of our sense of personal wholeness, meaning, or control.[17] None of us is spared this reality. We know it whether it comes from pain and sickness, the death of friends and family, the loss of a job, loneliness, or the collapse of a dream such as living a long life or having a happy family. When we suffer, we lose our connection to God, to others, to our own identity, and to our sense of purpose in life. This sense of loss is heightened by a feeling of isolation from all those activities and people that once supported us.[18]

A compassionate ministry takes us out of the physical realm of medical attempts to alleviate pain or preserve health and into the metaphysical realm of human happiness or a meaningful life. This is the realm of philosophy, religion, and spirituality—the worlds of pastoral ministry. Clearly we ought not to glorify suffering or portray it as a value in itself. Suffering is not one of those problems in life that provokes the question, "How are we going to solve this?" Suffering, rather, poses a subtler question, "How do we behave toward it?" Compassion is the virtue that empowers us to behave toward suffering in ways that relieve what we can and that offer support to bear what we cannot relieve. As with all the virtues, compassion gets clarified by practice.

One compassionate way to behave toward suffering is the willingness to interrupt our routine and comfort so as to be with those who suffer in order to help them live with and through the suffering. It can take the concrete expression of providing religious symbols and rituals as a source of meaning and comfort. It can also take the form of meeting material needs such as finding a new doctor, or giving financial assistance, or modifying the sufferer's living environment. But whatever form it takes, compassionate behavior is not a one-time intervention limited to a specific instance of suffering. Compassion is the virtue of the long haul, not a quick fix. It is willing to go the distance with the sufferer as the process of suffering unfolds through various phases and as the needs of the sufferer change in the passing days, weeks, and months.

Another way of behaving toward suffering is to deepen our connectedness to others. Suffering tends to isolate. Compassion is the bridge that restores the suffering to their place in the community. Stanley Hauerwas captures it well when he says that for Christians, suffering cannot be separated from our commitment to community. Historically, Christians have not had a "solution" to the problem of suffering. Hauerwas says, "They have had a community of care that has made it possible for them to absorb the destructive terror of evil that constantly threatens to destroy all human relations."[19] The challenge to ministerial compassion is to bind the suffering and nonsuffering into the same caring community. Compassion is the virtue that enables ministers to get people involved with each other and responsible to and for one another. Through the cooperation of healthcare facilities, schools, churches, mosques, and synagogues, for example, we can provide an antidote to the isolation that threatens to cut off those who are suffering from a network of social support.

A third form of a compassionate ministry is attending to the spiritual dimensions of suffering. Being unable to integrate the experience of diminishment is true spiritual suffering. Our spiritual vision of life helps sustain a framework of meaning that supports our movement through the experience of suffering and enables us to respond in a way that bears witness to love. A story I once heard from a hospice nurse makes this point vivid. She spoke of how she used a small, plain wooden cross, like the Franciscan Tau cross, that fit into the palm of the hand so that it could be gripped when someone was afraid. At such times, sensory identification with the suffering of Jesus enabled the patient to experience emotionally—not simply affirm intellectually—that another has known our fear of death. In this mode of caring, patients may more easily feel connected to one who understands, and they may not feel so alone. Compassionate care like this keeps a person connected to communities of shared meaning wherein they find affirmation and consolation as they confront the fundamental ambiguity of their condition.

But virtuous "suffering with" is not always a matter of doing something to relieve the suffering. As Daniel Callahan has pointed out in his book, *The Troubled Dream of Life*, there is a more subtle dimension of compassion than relieving the burden of suffering. It is not to focus on trying to explain suffering but to be present, often in silence and helplessness, to the one who suffers. It is like the friends of Job before they tried to explain things through their theology. As the text says, "They sat with him on the ground seven days and seven nights, and no one spoke a word to him, for they saw that his suffering was very great" (Job 2:13). When suffering cannot be overcome, compassion takes the form of accepting the suffering that another must endure. Such may be the case when the suffering comes from courageously standing up for one's convictions, or when parents suffer by accepting their children's need to make their own mistakes. In instances like these, compassion partners with patience, fidelity, and courage to suffer with the other.[20]

The virtue of compassion in ministry must reach beyond the one-to-one connection of caregiver and victim and into the collective dimension as well.[21] For example, compassion can exhibit a particular sensitivity toward and generate responsiveness to certain kinds of people or against specific social problems—immigrants, the homeless, persons with AIDS, oppressed minorities, racism, and sexism, for example. Compassion is related to our sense of justice and courage when it helps us to learn how certain unjust conditions or policies hurt particular groups and then leads us to do something about it.

As the core virtue expressing the social vision of Jesus' dream of God's reign, compassion aims at alleviating suffering caused by social structures and at changing whatever structures and policies need to be changed so that there aren't so many victims. A compassionate ministry ought to be a leaven of compassion both in the church and in the world. A compassionate ministry raises consciousness about the social vision of our biblical tradition and about the way social structures impact people's lives today. Compassion in ministry realizes that how we structure ourselves and the policies we live by are central to our becoming a more compassionate church and society.

Some practices that cultivate and express compassion are:

- being with another in whatever he or she is enduring without blame, judgment, or projection of one's own preoccupations;
- practicing a corporal work of mercy;
- listening attentively to the meaning of what another is experiencing;
- following through on promises and commitments to be with and for others;
- being present to the evening news and letting the circumstances of others move our hearts and maybe even bring us to tears;
- working with the poor, alienated, and disadvantaged.

## Generosity

Generosity follows closely behind compassion on the list of virtues necessary for ministry by those in my workshops—a good sign. For while it is true that everyone is expected to be generous as part of practicing Christian charity, ministers are expected to be even more so. We should not be surprised to be criticized for a lack of character when people experience us as showing undue concern for ourselves instead of being available and ready to serve them. Ministers who are more faithful to their regimen at the gym than they are in meeting pastoral needs are a case in point. As ministers, we are expected to be magnanimous, to make ourselves available to others and, in the biblical idiom, to be willing to "go the extra mile."

Generosity is the virtue of giving—the opposite of selfishness. Whoever is not generous is petty, stingy, and greedy. In contrast to justice, which is giving to others what is their due, generosity is giving to others what is ours. When we think of generosity, however, the first place our minds go to is what we do with our money. We think of everything from the simplest act of tossing a buck in the bucket of the panhandler in front of the bank to the philanthropic grant awarded by a foundation with a large endowment. It is easy to be critical of those who have money and want to challenge them to do more. We judge those without money as innocent victims of those who have it. Generally people in ministry do not rank among the wealthy in the United States. But this is no license to condemn moneyed people.

Financial wealth has always been met with some ambivalence among Christians. In the wisdom tradition of the Old Testament, wealth is a sign of blessing and evidence that one is living properly (Eccl 5:19; Ps 112:3). The prophets, however, especially Amos, pronounce a judgment on the wealthy for their complacent self-indulgence (Amos 6:1-7). By contrast, the gospels show that Jesus did not disdain wealth as such. In fact, he numbered some wealthy among his companions (Matt 4:21; Mark 15:41; Luke 10:38; John 19:38-39) and enjoyed the hospitality of Zacchaeus, a rich man who did not let his wealth be an obstacle to his salvation (Luke 19:1-10). The Synoptic Gospels, however, clearly recognize the dangers of wealth when they all teach that it is easier for a camel to go through the eye of a needle than for the rich to enter the kingdom of God (Matt 9:24; Mark 10:25; Luke 18:25). What really counts about wealth in the teaching of Jesus is not whether we have it but how we use it. Jesus taught that we can see our real priorities when we look at how we spend our money ("For where your treasure is, there your heart will be also"; Matt 6:21) and that we can test our true faithfulness to God by our attitude toward money ("No one can serve two masters. . . . You cannot serve God and wealth"; Matt 6:24).

What the gospels do condemn is greed—the unwillingness to share.[22] The greedy grab what they can, hoard it for their own use, and shut others out. The writings of Luke are especially poignant on this matter. In the story of the Rich Fool, the farmer is held up as the paragon of greed for hoarding all of his produce; in the story of the Rich Man and Lazarus, the rich man is condemned for not sharing his wealth (Luke 16:19-31); the Rich Ruler could not inherit eternal life because he could not bring himself to distribute his money to the poor (Luke 18:18-25). Ananias and Sapphira were struck dead for not sharing with the community (Acts 5:1-11), but Zacchaeus is praised for putting his money in service of the needy (Luke 19:1-10) and the widow is praised for being generous with the little that she had (Luke 21:1-4). The underlying assumption of these stories is pithily put by St. Paul's famous expression, "The love of money is a root of all kinds of evil" (1 Tim 6:10).

My favorite gospel reminder to be generous is in Matthew's account of Jesus' instructions to his apostles before sending them on their first missionary journey: "You received without payment; give without payment" (Matt 10:8). He tells them, in effect, "Be generous!" A friend of mine once gave me as a gift an ink drawing of a woman holding a small bird in her hand. It comes with an inscription that loosely translates Jesus' instructions: "The gift you have been given, give as gift." I value this image and inscription as a reminder to be generous. When we recognize that what we have comes to us more as gift than as achievement, then we can give freely what we have received freely. Generosity flows from gratitude. Not to be generous is to be ungrateful. In the spirit of the psalmist, generosity asks, "What shall I return to the LORD for all his bounty to me?" (Ps 116:12) I rephrase this prayer as, "What will I do with what I have? Hold on to it tightly, or share it?" The bird sitting in open hands reminds me to keep a loose grip on all that is given to me. It makes it easier to give things away. In using what we have to serve the community, we are giving as gift what we have received as gift.

The take-home message from the gospel stories about wealth is that greed, as an excessive attachment to money and to what money can buy, is a great obstacle to the freedom to live as a disciple of Jesus, to imitate the generosity of God, and to create bonds of unity within the community. Generosity, by contrast, as detachment from material wealth, frees us for responding to the demands of discipleship and the community's needs. Where greed is callous toward those in want, generosity is sensitive to what will build up our life together. These stories challenge us to think about our spending habits and what they tell us about our attachments. Is our life centered on acquiring more stuff? Have we become tightfisted about what we have? Or do we keep a loose grip that makes it easier to share? If others knew nothing else about us but our patterns of getting and giving, what sort of person would they know? Do we consider our true wealth to lie in what we have or in what we share?

But generosity as a virtue is about more than what we do with our financial wealth. The challenge of living generously is to see wealth more broadly to include our talents, our time, and our space. Generosity is also about giving of oneself, doing our best when we are called to serve and doing so with an open heart. Wealth in all its dimensions is part of who we are. It is not separate from our spiritual and moral life. We measure how generous we really are not by the percentage we give away, but by the way we give what we have. The mark of a virtue, remember, is that it is a natural part of who we are. The tests of the authenticity of our generosity are whether giving is easy and enjoyable and not an onerous duty and whether it frees us for service or makes us anxious and preoccupied with protecting what we have acquired.

One of the best examples of generosity as a virtue that has to do with more than our spending habits is portrayed in the film, *Pay it Forward*. A twelve-year-old schoolboy, Trevor McKinney, is given a social studies project at school. He has to come up with a plan that would create social change through direct action. On his way home from school, Trevor notices a homeless man and decides to bring him home to feed him and to give him a place to stay until he can get on his feet again. That is when he devises the plan to "pay it forward." He would do a good deed for three people who must in turn each do good deeds for three other people. The plan becomes contagious. It begins a movement that has grown nationwide.[23]

Our acts of generosity may not receive the public acclaim that inaugurates a social movement of sharing, but they still have the power to point to a deeper reality governing our lives. Generosity reflects the very character of God as self-giving love. The central symbol of God in the Christian faith, God is love (1 John 4:8 and 16), has been spelled out in the doctrine of the Trinity. This doctrine is normative for understanding who God is and who we are to be as images of God. About God, the doctrine asserts a relationship of mutual self-giving: God is eternally a giver or lover (Father), the receiver or beloved (Son), and the gift of love that binds them together (Spirit). About us, the doctrine affirms that we are essentially social and made to share. We cannot properly express ourselves as images of God without being in relationship with others and sharing our gifts for the sake of each person and the whole community. To be made in the image of God is an imperative calling us to generosity and justice—to live out of the fullness of the gifts we have received by putting them to use for the good of the community.

Generosity that imitates God in pastoral ministry does not reduce fulfilling our professional responsibilities to meeting the minimum requirements of some prior agreement. Generosity is open to the unexpected and not just to our best laid plans. It motivates us to "go the extra mile" and not to be puny with our presence or our service. Generosity is the habit of using our knowledge, power, and position in ways that will give greater preference to the needs of the other over our own. It makes some personal sacrifices of time and attention by changing plans if necessary, even if that might cause us some inconvenience. Generosity is the energy of being hospitable. It creates a place where others can come in and experience new bonds of communion because they have found someone who has room for them, accepts them as they are, and does not try to impose plans on them, manipulate them, or control them. Generosity also tries to make things work out so that everyone wins.

Without generosity, everyone who seeks our pastoral service will be seen as an opportunity for self-gain rather than as someone in need. But with generosity, we are free enough to delay pursuing our own interests in favor of self-disciplined service to the community. Generosity like this makes little sense in a world where self-interest trumps service. But it makes a world of sense when put in the context of faith. We are called to imitate God's generosity of self-giving love, and to imitate Christ in his special feeling for those in need.

But, as with any virtue, generosity can be lost to its extremes. At one extreme is the greedy miser, like Ebenezer Scrooge, who only causes misery for others by hoarding gifts that could be a source of liberation and healing if shared. At the other extreme is the profligate prodigal who wastes wealth by reckless extravagance. Beware of what might look like generosity in its unsparing bounty. It can actually be a form of subtle manipulation in disguise. Those who are generous to a fault may unknowingly or, what is worse, purposefully play on another's dependence to win admiration and acceptance, to advance their own interests, or to gain recognition. Finding the mean between these extremes is not always easy for ministers whose temptation is to be more rather than less generous.

Generosity as a virtue needs its boundaries. The appropriate expression of generosity will be found when it partners with justice, fidelity, and self-care. Giving out of our gifts is not generous when we undermine the common good by serving one segment of the community to the exclusion of another, when we overwhelm the pastoral relationship by drowning the other with codependent care, or when we harm ourselves by overreaching our limits of time, energy, or personal resources. If we can honor our own needs for healthy living, then we may be able to model that same self-regard for others. To know where to draw the line on what generosity demands requires the keen moral sensibilities of the virtue of prudence.

How we use our wealth in all its dimensions reflects our sense of responsibility to and for the community. By sharing what we have to enhance life, we imitate the generosity of God. By hoarding it, we erode the virtue of generosity and ignore the claims of justice.

Some practices that cultivate and express generosity are:

- taking care of ourselves by maintaining our physical, emotional, social, and spiritual health;
- giving away two items of clothing we haven't worn in two years;
- responding with reasonable preference for the interests of others even if it means sacrificing some of our own;
- being approachable as well as available to help people;
- making a donation to a charitable organization;
- volunteering to help the disadvantaged, such as with Habitat for Humanity;
- anticipating others' needs and how they will be affected by our own actions.

## Courage

Courage is the apex of character. It is the virtue universally admired for protecting and promoting the dignity of conscience and personal integrity. Rooted in the Latin word for "heart," *cor*, courage is the disposition to act with lots of heart. This implies both an authenticity in expressing ourselves and a wholeness of the affective, physical, and cognitive aspects of ourselves. We know courage perhaps better in its slang synonyms: spirit, moxie, gumption, guts, backbone, and nerve. All allude to having the strength to do something that is dangerous and comes with a price tag of no small cost and often draws the disapproval of others but that we feel is worth the risk if we are to be true to ourselves. Courage impels us to act.

On the one hand, it keeps us from being paralyzed by fear so we never take risks (cowardice or timidity). On the other hand, it protects us from becoming so reckless in our confidence that we will be safe no matter what (foolhardiness).

Since the ancients, courage, in its fullest sense, has been associated with the willingness to die. For Aristotle the paradigm of courage was the soldier on the battlefield.[24] For Thomas Aquinas, martyrdom holds primacy of place as an exemplary act of Christian courage.[25] If the willingness to die is a quality exhibited only by soldiers and martyrs, then the rest of us can marvel at it, but the vast majority of us need hardly worry about ever practicing it. To be courageous in everyday life we need to expand the meaning of facing death.

Everyday courage helps us face the fear of anything that threatens us. One of my favorite profiles in everyday courage comes from *To Kill a Mockingbird*. After Jem destroys Mrs. Dubose's camellia bushes in retaliation of her racist slurs and general meanness toward the Finches, Atticus devises a punishment for him. As reparation, Jem must visit the old woman in her home to read to her—every day for a month. When Mrs. Dubose dies shortly after the month is up, Atticus reveals to Jem that she was addicted to morphine and that the reading was part of her effort to conquer her addiction, a fight that wins Atticus's highest praise for courage. He says to Jem:

> I wanted you to see what real courage is, instead of getting the idea that courage is a man with a gun in his hand. It's when you know you're licked before you begin but you begin anyway and you see it through no matter what. You rarely win, but sometimes you do. Mrs. Dubose won, all ninety-eight pounds of her. According to her views, she died beholden to nothing and nobody. She was the bravest person I ever knew.[26]

In the midst of all of our diverse ministries, we face threats to our safety in various ways, even though we don't physically lose our lives. We need courage to persevere amid adversity. For example, we all have a Mrs. Dubose or two in our lives. We all have to deal with difficult people whose racist, sexist, or elitist attitude contaminates our work environments and whose actions undermine our best efforts to make life better for everyone. We also face malicious rumors that threaten to ruin our reputations, and we face the intimidations of someone more powerful than we are. Sometimes we have to speak candidly to the pastor or the bishop at risk of losing our job, or confront a colleague about misconduct. We have to move on after a successful tenure as a pastor or teacher and resist the temptation to interfere with those who replace us when they change everything we worked so hard to establish. We sometimes struggle with the tension between being an officer of the church and being our own person. We meet unexpected events that bring us face to face with our limits, such as our personal inadequacies of knowledge, skill, or energy. We get sick, we grow older and weaker, and we all face death. There's plenty to be afraid of, but we don't let it stop us. If we are not going to let our fears and threats do us in, then we need courage, both physical and moral.

When we are threatened with bodily harm, we need physical courage. This is the courage that enables a minister to walk into the sick room, for example, to sit with and even to touch patients without being paralyzed by fear of contracting a disease. But when the threat is to something we value, such as our job, reputation, friendship, integrity, or self-esteem, then we need moral courage: a heartfelt commitment to the values that define who we are and what we believe life is about.

The defining characteristic of courage in ministry is less likely to be physical courage than moral courage—the ability to be our own person and to stand up for what we believe. Moral courage is the courage that promotes integrity. We find it in the prophet, the social reformer, or the corporate whistleblower. Witness to moral courage is what I think so many of us admired in Rosa Parks and Martin Luther King Jr. as they fought nonviolently for civil rights. Moral courage enabled Sojourner Truth to campaign against slavery and for women's rights. It compelled Dorothy Day to stand against violence and for the poor. We admire these people for having the courage to be their own person and to act on the strength of their convictions. They did not trim their sails to the prevailing winds and end up saying or doing only what would win approval. They did what they believed was right about life in spite of the risk of rejection or ridicule. With Atticus Finch, they knew "the one thing that doesn't abide by majority rule is a person's conscience."[27] When we measure our lives against people like these, we hope that we will never have to admit that, when a question of injustice came to us, we didn't have the courage to address it.

Three elements define moral courage: fear in the face of a threat; a willingness to endure danger; and standing up for the values that we say we live by.[28]

We know when a situation requires courage because we can feel the fear in our bodies—perspiration beads on our foreheads; our hands, filmed with sweat, clench tightly; our skin crawls; butterflies flutter in our stomach; our bowels rumble; we shiver; our knees tremble. Our whole body has the mental wish to run the other way. But, in the idiom of John Wayne, the courageous are those who may be shaking in their boots and scared to death, but they saddle up anyway.[29] To be courageous is not the same as having no fear. Fearlessness, in fact, is one of the extremes of the mean of courage. It is based on a false reading of the real danger in the situation, or it is based on a false confidence—the misreading of one's ability to handle it. Courage finds its way between the extremes of the foolhardy bravado of fearlessness (the irrationality that does not calculate how best to proceed on the basis of insight, imagination, and consultation) and cowering cowardice (the timidity that does not stand up for our convictions for fear of making a mistake or of offending someone). Courageous people carefully consider the dangers, but they do not let keeping safe from harm always win. Courage presupposes that we are afraid to face what threatens us; but, according to Josef Pieper, "its essence lies not in knowing no fear, but in not allowing oneself to be forced into evil by fear, or to be kept by fear from the realization of good."[30]

If fear of some danger is the first characteristic of moral courage, then the second is the willingness to hang in there when doing so is hard. Courage perseveres. Enduring danger is difficult because we know the cost is great. We may lose our job, our reputation, or even our life. Turning away from danger when the going gets rough only erodes whatever courage we may be bringing to face the danger. When courage collapses, we put ourselves at risk of selling out to those who shout the loudest or simply hold positions of power. If we sell out, then we are on the road to resigning ourselves to living with injustice and allowing immoral people, policies, and structures to prevail. Living with a steadfast "in spite of" in the face of obstacles to our fidelity or threats to our safety shows a confidence that the life of discipleship can be lived under the hope of resurrection. St. Teresa of Avila captures this expression of courage by making it a prerequisite for growing in holiness: "An imperfect human being needs more courage to pursue the way of perfection than suddenly to become a martyr."[31] Such perseverance is quite different from lip-biting obstinacy. Whereas obstinacy refuses to admit having made a wrong turn and so does not change even when reason shows the need to, perseverance, or endurance, keeps its eye on the good we are committed to. It continues to be creative in expressing discipleship so as to avoid falling into a rut that fails to meet the demands of changing times.

We are able to persevere because of the third element of moral courage—a heartfelt commitment to value. One of the dangers of not standing for what we believe to be true is that we may fall for anything. If we fall for anything, we risk losing our soul. But neither would we be acting courageously to seek a change in policies and practices if we rushed recklessly into speaking truth to power. Courage is the virtue of appropriate fear and confidence seeking to do what is right. But it does not work alone. Courage is not only a condition of every virtue but also a virtue that engages other virtues:[32] self-esteem to know that we are rooted in love and cannot lose God's love (cf. Rom 8:38-39), humility to know our limits, generosity to act selflessly, justice and compassion to compel our desire for good and to focus our passion, and prudence to discern our way between the extremes of being cowardly or foolhardy.

Moral courage protects our integrity because it enables us to act on what we believe really matters. In this way, courage is the virtue that helps to define us because it upholds the dignity of personal conscience. Our conscience is the ultimate court of appeal once we have done the hard work of forming it. We let our integrity suffer and slip into inauthenticity when we allow any person, institution, or authority to replace conscience in the name of being loyal or obedient. More than one pastoral minister has shared with me the tension they feel when caught between an official position of the church and the reality of their own pastoral experience and insight gained from prayer, study, and serious reflection. Taking a stand in the name of conscience is not stubbornly clinging to the familiar and the comfortable, but it is witnessing to integrity. Acting with the courage of our convictions is the well-earned prerogative of those who follow through with their responsibility to discover what is right and good, identify with it, and become willing to pay the price for being so committed.

To uphold courage as a virtue for ministry that protects personal integrity is to encourage everyone to have the courage to be their own person. Instead of submitting unquestioningly to authority, we commit ourselves to coming to greater clarity on where we stand and why we stand there. Living with the courage of our convictions does not mean that we have to have a fully articulate position on every controversial moral or political issue that arises—war in the Middle East, stem cell research, gay marriage, healthcare reform, capital punishment, abortion, euthanasia, etc.—but we ought to be committed to discovering what really matters to us rather than to clinging only to what is safest or most acceptable to others. We cannot claim to have integrity if we act simply on the basis of what someone else says we ought to do.

If there is one lesson that the stories of courageous people have taught us it is that we cannot run from our fears except at great cost to ourselves. Just as we do not become courageous by making one bold move, so we do not lose courage in one instance. It withers away, bit by bit. Small betrayals driven by the fear of losing acceptance or approval, especially of those in authority, erode courage. Courage deteriorates when we fail to think critically, remain silent before an issue we deeply care about, or allow something to continue that we know to be wrong. These kinds of avoidances weaken courage because they make us comfortable hiding behind our fears when, in the image of John Wayne, "saddling up" and taking fear along for the ride would be more costly. Before we know it, we become compromised. We have lost our soul. But having the courage to face everyday tests of our integrity helps us to determine how we will respond when we come face to face with a significant moment of truth.

Courage, like the other virtues, is a habit we acquire by practice.[33] Since courage depends on our ability to pay the price when we act on our convictions, we need to strengthen our capacity for sacrifice. To cultivate courage we need to engage in ascetical practices that nurture our ability to let go, such as the disciplines of fasting, almsgiving, and solitude. Courage also requires the inner honesty of critical self-knowledge that comes from a periodic examination of conscience and making a life review. Through these exercises we can learn from our failures by recognizing previous less-than-courageous actions and admit that we could have chosen otherwise but let fear get the upper hand. We also need to exercise our creative imagination to envision what courage must look like. Praying imaginatively with Scripture stories can train the imagination to project ourselves into different scenarios to see how it feels to take a risk, to be rejected, to distinguish real and false dangers, and to live with the disciples.

Since courage only shows itself in the face of a threat, these practices are ways to prepare ourselves to be courageous when the threat arises:

- reading some biographies or memoirs of courageous people;

- clarifying our convictions by talking about what really
  matters to us with someone with whom we feel safe;
- making a regular examination of conscience to learn from
  our failures in courage;
- engaging in some ascetical practice that trains us in letting
  go of some good;
- volunteering an opinion when it is not supported by the
  majority.

Every ministerial activity has a pastoral dimension because each
in its own way shapes the life of the community. Pastoral ministry
is how the church carries out its mission to be a sign of God's saving
presence in the world and to be an agent of uniting all peoples with
God and with one another. The virtues for developing pastorally
enable us to move out of ourselves so that we can build up relationships that will give people the vision and hope to face the challenges
of life. Justice is foundational to this end for it governs the ties that
bind us; compassion softens our individuality by enabling us to
share in another's feelings of suffering and then reaching out to do
what we can to relieve it; generosity drives our service by giving
our time, talents, and treasure; courage makes it possible to serve
with integrity in the face of pressures to compromise our convictions or to hide behind our fears. These virtues are integral to the
service we give that enables the church to make present God's saving care for all peoples.

❈  ❈  ❈  ❈

Such is my vision of a morally integrated spirituality for pastoral
ministers. But, you may be asking, "Where can I meet this virtuoso?" While I drew these virtues from my observation of various
pastoral ministers who are regarded as models of a good minister,
I am not claiming that any one person embodies all of these virtues
fully, or excellently. Nor do I claim that anyone in ministry is mor-

ally blameworthy for not developing these virtues in an excellent way. We are not required to be heroines, heroes, or saints in order to be good or holy. But we are required to look in that direction. The ideal of virtuous living remains our goal toward which we ought to direct ourselves, however gradually. We always ought to have our hearts and minds set on improving our character. One of the characteristics of virtue ethics is that it is concerned with the process of ongoing conversion. It takes us where we are, gives us a vision of the kind of person we can aim to become, describes the habits we need to get there, and it inspires us to set ourselves in the direction of that goal, even if we never become fully that kind of person.

There are a variety of ways to configure these virtues with different degrees of emphasis and development. The communion of saints testifies to a variety of ways to live our spirituality. St. John Vianney (the Cure d'Ars) was not Oscar Romero, and the Little Flower was not Dorothy Day. Each models goodness and holiness in different ways. These foregoing chapters have tried only to set out the qualities of character that I think are necessary for ministry though not sufficient if we are to be sacraments of Christ and agents of God's reign of peace and unity among all peoples and with the earth.

I am very much aware that commending any list of virtues invites others to ask why this list rather than others. Any list underwrites a certain conception of what counts for an "excellent" minister. You may want to add a few of your own or drop a few of mine. You may also have different interpretations of the virtues in my list. The specific meaning of a virtue can change over time and in different cultures. Virtues, remember, are not action-specific and depend on the community's vision of the good. How we express a virtue depends a great deal on our culture, personality, maturity, and the context in which we live. Analogies are always possible, but there will also be differences in how we exemplify the virtue. For example, the courage of the soldier facing enemy fire is different from the courage of the pastoral associate who must speak truth to the power of the pastor or bishop, or of the bishop who must confront one of his priests about professional misconduct, or of the pastor who must rein in a difficult staff person.

Furthermore, you may have noticed some overlap in my description of the virtues. This is not unusual since there are no hard barriers between the behaviors that belong to each virtue or between the four areas in which I have organized them. The four areas flow together, influencing and reinforcing one another in an ongoing process that is more like energy fields than pillars of the Parthenon. So too is it with the virtues. They are interconnected and do not exist in isolation from one another. We cannot understand generosity, for example, without justice, compassion, and courage. The virtues support and strengthen each other. Their interconnection implies that virtuous acts will be acts of more than one virtue, and the strength of the virtuous act, generosity for example, will be compromised in a person who is short on those virtues with which it is connected.

I hope this spirituality for pastoral ministers has stimulated your own thinking of the kind of minister you want to become in serving the mission of the church. Achieving excellence in ministry requires a host of virtues working together to give coherence, direction, and wholeness to our lives as disciples modeled after Jesus, our paradigm of the virtuous minister. Our remaining task is to describe what will help us along the way to goodness and holiness.

# What Will Help Us along the Way?

# 6

# Becoming Good, Becoming Holy

Thus far we have undertaken quite a journey. The guiding conviction that has steered us along the way is that our spirituality manifests itself in our character traits and style of life. By following the way of goodness and holiness along the path of virtue, we have been able to see that a morally integrated spirituality in the ministerial life entails at least being grateful for grace, being committed to searching for truth and acting on it, being compassionate in terms of desiring the betterment of others in need, being generous with our blessings, being courageous in terms of risking self-interest, and the like. The remaining task is to unpack the aids that will help us along the way. These are community, friendship, mentors and models, and spiritual practices.

## Community

The path we have followed shows that the way of goodness and holiness inextricably binds us to others. We form our own character in interdependent relationships with others. The key to forming character for ministry is to participate in a community of people with good character who can model for us what being good and being holy look like. There is no other way to know what constitutes virtuous behavior than from within a community whose conception of the good creates such people and promotes them in its choice of heroes, its honors bestowed, and its recognition of moral authority. Virtues need to be demonstrated, not just described. Only by participating in the life of the community that produces and preserves virtues will we be able to understand them.[1]

Over the years, as I look back over my studies of how we acquire character, one important lesson has emerged: forming character is a cooperative adventure. We do not acquire character on our own. I have vivid memories of growing up with our extended family, which met frequently for backyard fun at various members' homes. I remember mom or dad announcing, as the last car pulled into the driveway, "The gang's all here!" Surrounded by the "gang" I learned about generosity and stinginess, hospitality and alienation, fair play and cheating. While no one member of the family embodied any one or all of these traits fully, collectively the family portrayed the kind of person I wanted to be or not, and I knew that I was in the company of people who could help me get there.

Social scientists tell us that, as we grow, the character we acquire is in part the result of internalizing the beliefs and values, causes and loyalties of the communities that make up our environment. Values belong to the group before they belong to the individual.[2] Family, school, and church have long played a primary role in being a formative community. Today we should not forget to add the arts, the media, and especially the internet. The styles of life and systems of values that these worlds of influence communicate to us are quickly usurping, if they have not already overtaken, the role of family, school, and church in shaping character. Since we live in multiple communities that overlap and often compete with each other in their influence on character, we need to be able to assess critically the images of the good life that these various communities communicate. The challenge of forming character for ministry is to create and sustain communities that support virtues fitting for ministry and then trust the power of the group to teach individuals what it means to be that sort of person.

Sociologist James Davidson Hunter has studied the moral cultures characterizing America and the role of those cultures in influencing the moral life. While social scientists typically name a range of factors, such as race, age, class, ethnicity, and gender to account for moral judgments, Hunter contends that the most important factor cutting across all of these is an underlying attachment to a moral culture.[3] Culture here means the patterns of meaning that a community develops to interpret and evaluate what is going on.[4] These patterns of meaning are not so much taught as caught by sharing in common practices, such as joining together in social service projects, having meals together, praying together, spending leisure time together, and sharing stories of our experiences to uncover their common meaning. Once these patterns of meaning get into our bloodstream, they predispose us toward certain feelings, dispositions, and actions.

The challenge of the sociological research to forming character is to ask how well we are facilitating an attachment to a Christian moral culture that shapes our imaginations. A morally integrated Christian spirituality grows best where Christian metaphors serve as the primary interpretive framework for making sense of life. When images of faith undergird the framework within which we interpret our experiences, they can become a great influence on our character and action. Our imaginations are shaped by these religious images as we participate in the life of the community and its spiritual practices. Both help us develop our relationships with one another and with God.

But we also need to be cautious about claiming too much for what a community's culture can do to shape character for ministry. Formation personnel are often held responsible for the quality of candidates and their ministry. While they do share some of the responsibility, formation personnel and programs are not as influential as many people think they are. Long before candidates enter schools of ministry and formation programs, their habit formation, and so character formation, is well advanced. As the aphorism has it, "How you start is how you finish." It is not unusual to see the character a candidate brings through the front door of a formation program to be, by and large, the very same character walking out the back door at the end of the process. Character does not go in reverse easily. The arc of conversion is long, not short. So we can expect that the kinds of habits we form prior to entering ministry to influence, more than we might want to admit, the kind of minister we will become and the style our ministry will take.

We can derive wisdom from another saying: "If we want to produce a gold ring, we had better begin with some gold ore." If candidates for ministry do not manifest habitual patterns indicating that they already possess an ability to live the style of life and to exercise the ministry for which they are being recruited and formed, then they should never be recruited for ministry in the first place. It is naïve (and nonsacramental) to think that ordination or commissioning will suddenly render someone capable of ministry. Theologically we would say, "grace builds on nature." The responsibility of the formation personnel is to fine tune those habits of the candidate that will enhance the ministry of the church and to challenge and try to reform those that handicap it. Some change may happen, but radical changes are rare. People generally stay "in character." Formation personnel generally dismiss atypical behavior or give it little attention because it is so uncharacteristic of the candidate's true self.

Beyond the community of our initial formation are other communities that continue to support ongoing formation and growth in virtue. For example, some ministers have peer support groups that meet regularly to review life and to affirm and challenge one another to grow in virtue. Priests often meet for study weeks or convocations that can provide a supportive environment to encourage growth in virtue. Ministerial colleagues, such as directors of religious education or permanent deacon cohorts, also meet regularly for retreats or to discuss common interests and challenges in their ministry and to support one another in needed virtues. The role of the community in forming virtue is an ongoing aide to virtue throughout our ministerial life. The challenge is to be sure we participate in communities that share a common vision of the good life and common goals of our spiritual journey.

## Friendship

Within the larger communities in which we live, there is a smaller circle of closer relationships that have a great influence on who we become. The people we talk to, what we talk about, and how we live together are the training ground for our character. So we need to watch the company we keep. Christian character formation requires that we develop stable, enduring relationships with those who share and try to live by a Christian perspective on life. We cannot become good on our own. We need relationships with people who also want to be good, who share our aspirations, and who love us enough to help us achieve them. These are our friends. Whatever strength of character we achieve is not the result of our own efforts alone. The handiwork of friends also draws the best out of us. [5]

Forming character for ministry requires friendships that grow out of that place in ourselves where we know that we are loved. But what so often passes for friendship today grows out of a need for attention and affirmation. What we call friendships are often superficial acquaintances or codependent relationships of manipulation. Friendships are also easily jeopardized by consumerism that believes newer is better or that we need things more than people. But, as the bumper sticker reminds us, "The best things in life are not things." In a consumer society, our identity is too easily measured by our riches and not by the richness of our love. We can too easily make friends into just another commodity to pick up, use, and dispose of as we see fit.

Our culture's ethos of individualism also militates against valuing friendship. It sees the self not as social and relational but as private, autonomous, and self-sufficient. Individualism suggests that the more independent we are, the better off we are, and that people are more likely to take life from us than to give it. In its most radical forms, individualism undermines the fundamental gift of friendship: assurance that each friend wants what is best for the other and will work to secure it.

Friendships are marked by mutual enjoyment of and care for one another, a desire for what is best for one another, the commitment to seek one another's well-being, and the freedom that allows for growth at each one's own pace. The company of good friends enlarges our imaginations. Our friends teach us how to be with and care for others by being genuinely empathic, loyal, just, generous and gracious. In other words, being friends with a few opens the imagination to ways of being friendly toward many. This is what friends do for each other. Candidates for ministry ought to be able to demonstrate their ability to build and sustain friendships.

To form character for ministry, what kind of friends do we need? According to Robert Wicks, we need people who can play a number of crucial roles: prophet, cheerleader, harasser, and spiritual guide.[6]

Friends who play the prophet challenge us when we let our priorities slip. Their prophetic voice tells us when we are accumulating too much—too much of ourselves, too much of our opinions, too much of our way. These are the friends who hold us accountable to our obligations and to what we profess as ministers of the Gospel.

The challenging voice of the prophetic friend must be balanced by the encouraging voice of the cheerleader. One of the great gifts of friendship is that friends help each other become more fully who they are called to be. Friends so get a kick out of seeing the handiwork of God in each other that their friendship frees them to be their best selves. As Wicks says of the cheerleader, "Burnout is always around the corner when we don't have people who are ready to encourage us, see our gifts clearly, and be there for us when our involvement with people, their sometimes unrealistic demands, and our own crazy expectations for ourselves, threaten to pull us down."[7] Our cheerleaders give us the security and the freedom we need to embrace the vocation entrusted to us.

The harasser friend is the one who helps us to face the danger of taking ourselves too seriously. Harassers help us to laugh at our situations and at ourselves and so gain perspective again.

Spiritual guides are friends who help us deal with our fears, especially the ones that undermine our trust in God's love for us. They help us appreciate the need for necessary detachments so that we can be free enough to create space in our lives for the people and opportunities God has given us to enjoy. Spiritual guides also help us to keep perspective on what is essential (relationships) and what isn't (concern with image, power, accomplishments). Spiritual guides like these can be mentors, spiritual directors, support groups, and even spiritual authors who open fresh attitudes toward life.

To survive in the world, we need food, clothing, and shelter. To survive in ministry, we need friends. Without them, ministry is a mission impossible.

## Mentors and Models

Within our communities of influence are certain individuals we notice who embody more clearly than others the virtues we want to develop and the character we want to imitate. These are our mentors and models. The mentoring relationship, the more formal of the two, is an intentional, time-limited apprenticeship to someone who embodies the kind of life to which we aspire. Under a mentor, we not only learn what to do through observation and instruction but also pick up the spirit of how to do it. My favorite example of mentoring is my mother teaching me to cook. "Watch so you'll learn" was her singular instruction. Standing at the head of her pasta board where she would mix, roll, and cut her pasta and bread dough, I watched. Then, from time to time, I touched in order to get the feel of the dough as it progressed through its various phases from flour, eggs, salt, and water to its silky finish. Then came her second instruction, "Now you do it." Doing it myself, over and over, made the mixing, kneading, and rolling become second nature to me.

Only through practice did I catch the nuances of feeling for the dough, a feeling that lives in my fingers and not in the recipe. In time, after much practice, I no longer need the recipe or my mentor. I am now good at it. I can be a mentor for the next generation who will also have to watch so as to learn.

To be a formative agent in ministerial life, mentoring requires not only the mentor's explicit attempt to pass on a vision and style of life but also the candidate's openness to receive it. No mentor is going to have an influence on anyone who is not open to being influenced.[8]

Modeling relationships, by contrast, are less formalized and are not as self-conscious. Modeling in ministerial formation illustrates the axioms, "good people form good people," and, "witness is more compelling than argument." Arguments do not instill virtue. Someone must capture our imaginations and, by so doing, open us to a world of possibility. The virtues discussed as forming the way to goodness and holiness are embodied by real models in ministry. Our models are the ones who make true the sayings, "Your actions speak so loud, I can't hear what you say," and "It's not what you say; it's who you are," and "Example is the best teacher." Their characters so fascinate us that our models capture our imaginations and move us to want to be like them.

The importance of models to inspire us came home to me clearly in a conversation I had with a group of priests talking about what drew us to the priesthood in the first place. To a man, it wasn't any idea about priesthood, or an in-depth knowledge of the meaning of a religious vocation. Knowledge supporting our vocations came later. In the beginning was witness—Fr. Jerry, Fr. Ed, Fr. Bill, real, living, flesh-and-blood priests who inspired us. They lived with an energy that was infectious in its attractiveness. They ministered with a confident competence that nurtured a desire to want to be like them. We said to ourselves, in effect, "If this way of life can produce someone like that, then I want to be part of what he has."

Different models pass by us before we decide, "I'll be a priest," or "I'll study theology because I want to be like Dr. Smith, my theology professor." Models are important because they become "norms" for us. So we watch them like hawks to see how it's done. We are drawn to the goals of one, the style of another, the spirit of a third. We watch them "doing their thing" and learn from them the skills that make them worthy of imitation. Through a process of observation and imitation we begin to develop a character like theirs.

Robert Coles captures the dynamic of personal witness well in his experience of becoming a doctor:

> I remember myself as a young doctor, and as a witness to that elder doctor.　.　.　. He didn't give lectures and sermons as to how we interns and residents ought to behave with one another, with the hospital staff, with the children we were treating. Nor were we handed articles to read.　.　.　. In fact, he *said* very little to us; he lived out his moral principles, and soon enough, we were witnesses to his behavior, to his ways of being with others, which we were challenged to absorb, as all young people are inclined to do, when they have learned to admire and trust someone older: try to follow suit.[9]

What Coles seems to be telling us is that to become good, we need to be surrounded by goodness, to witness it, and then to imitate it.

Teachers and formation personnel beware! We capture the imagination of candidates to ministry with our character and style. There is something about us that they want (or not) for themselves. Whether we want to do so or not, we teach virtue (or vice) in everything we say or do. In a formation community, the identity and integrity of the formation personnel, whether ordained, religious, or lay, figure more prominently than the content of the curriculum of study. We are formed more by the impact a particular person has on us than we are by the content of subject matter (though that also has formative influence when it gets us to reflect on virtues we need to cultivate and how a virtue is associated with emotions and manifest in attitudes and actions). Apart from formation communities, other ministers are models too—the pastor, the religious education teacher, the youth minister, a chaplain. Often without knowing it, they are being watched closely by those who want to know what the Christian life ought to look like, and, in being so watched, they are influencing the character of others more than they know.

The dynamics of observation and imitation in the formation of character are so strong that we who are involved in ministerial formation also need to be vigilant of the value system we express in the school, for institutions have character too. If we talk about collaboration, we need to be collaborators; if we advocate inclusiveness, we need to include difference in the community. Formation communities should see themselves as the conscious public practice of the virtues we profess to be necessary for ministry.

But simply surrounding candidates with good models is no guarantee that anyone will become good. Modeling is effective as a means of forming character when candidates are ready to learn from their models and are motivated to imitate what they see because they find their model's behavior desirable for themselves. They find themselves saying, "Yes. That's the way I want to be, too." Every candidate seeking to form character for ministry needs to witness and then to imitate moral models of ministry. What they learn through these models about themselves and about relating to others will have effects far beyond the boundaries of this special relationship.

We live in a big world where there are many people competing for a privileged place in our imaginations. But there is only one who is the exemplary image of Christian moral character. The whole Christian tradition points to Jesus as the paradigm of virtue.[10] As paradigm, Jesus is our primary example for what a minister's character ought to look like. He is the master. We are the disciples. As I tried to show in chapter 1, a goal of our spiritual journey is to conform our lives to his, not by copying his life point for point, but by harmonizing our lives with his by way of analogous behavior.[11]

We can be fascinated by Jesus the way we are fascinated by role models arising out of our families, friends, and formation community. A major difference, however, is that we physically interact with our family, friends, teachers, and formation directors. We see them and talk to them in the flesh. When it comes to Jesus, we have access to him through the gospels which tell his story. So the spiritual practice of praying with Scripture is an essential discipline in the formation of ministerial character. We believe that by prayerfully and imaginatively engaging these stories under the power of the Spirit and in the life of the church, we will be able to capture their meaning and so imitate Jesus in our day in ways that are consonant with his life in his day. Praying with Scripture in order to encounter Christ leads to my last aide along the way to goodness and holiness—the discipline of engaging in spiritual practices.

## Spiritual Practices

Spiritual practices have a great potential to shape our lives around Christian attitudes and values. We have already met this aid as the virtue of piety under the area of developing spiritually. Every ministerial formation program includes opportunities to engage in spiritual practices—private prayer, Mass, devotions, retreats, fasting, etc. As I claimed in chapter 1, we engage in spiritual practices primarily to show our love for God and to deepen our relationship with God. They are truly acts of worship, first of all. Their morally formative aspect is an indirect effect. William Spohn is emphatic on this point: "If the intent of worship is not God but personal growth, then God is being reduced to a means, which is a form of idolatry."[12]

While maintaining the priority of spiritual practices to express our love for God, the way of goodness and holiness is also interested in their potential in forming character. Prayer, both personal and communal, is the most obvious practice to express our spirituality. Cultivating the habit of prayer provides a place for us consciously to connect with God and to begin to see our whole life in relation to God and under the care of God. By attending to God in prayer, we gain a greater sensitivity to the presence of God in our midst and to what stands in the way of God, such as injustice and exploitation. As we draw closer to God and become more sensitive to what opposes God, we gain a compassion that includes more and more people. Our moral lives take on a different tone and quality as we become more aware of others and committed to caring for one another and the world. Over time, through our prayerful disciplines, we discover that we are forming dispositions befitting the attentiveness of a prayerful person—trusting, humble, reverent, open, grateful, compassionate, and the like.[13]

Praying with Scripture can become a way of schooling the emotions so that we are drawn to care about what disciples ought to care about, and it can sharpen our perspective and nudge us closer to seeing from God's point of view. Prayerful reflection on the parables, for example, can develop openness to the unexpected and a sense of humor that will catch the incongruous as an epiphany of grace. Savoring a word or image from Scripture can stir feelings within us that nurture attitudes (gratitude, compassion) and that move us to act in a way that expresses these interior dispositions (by saying "Thanks" for a favor received, or by spending time with a sick friend). Walking around inside biblical images and the emotions that arise from them can help us discover new ways of being faithful to what discipleship demands of us.

Prayers of petition and intercession can strengthen our capacity for solidarity, empathy, and compassion. Through these prayer forms, we confess our dependence and admit that we are not self-sufficient and that we are not alone. When we pray for others, we identify with them and their needs. But these prayers are not attempts to escape social responsibility by turning over to God what we do not want to have to face. Rather, by placing human need under the care of God, we are not only expressing our interdependence with others but also committing ourselves to assume responsibility to bring about that for which we pray. If we pray for peace, for example, we commit ourselves not only to trying not to be a source of conflict but also to forgiving those who have hurt us and to becoming instruments of reconciliation wherever we are. If we pray for a friend who is depressed but we never speak an encouraging word to him, then we are not praying "in Christ" in the fullest sense and living into that for which we pray. Our prayers not only express our spirituality—that is, our relation and dependence on God—they also give direction to our moral life.

The Eucharist can strengthen our religious identity and nurture our dispositions to gratitude, forgiveness, and solidarity. Paul Wadell answers the title question of his article, "What do all those Masses do for us?" by saying that they form us into persons with a new vision that opens us to the attitudes and virtues of Jesus.[14] The eucharistic imagination envisions a community of forgiveness, mutual respect, and self-giving love. Participating in the Eucharist can play a role in shaping the way we envision life and our role in it because the images we find in gathering as community, confessing our sins, hearing the word, professing a common faith, and sharing a common food can help us identify with the vision and values reflected in these ritual actions to make them our interpretive framework for discerning the direction of our lives. What we enact ritually around the eucharistic table is the way we ought to live when away from the table. We can see how celebrating the Eucharist is having a formative influence on our moral lives when we are able to be as hospitable and liberating toward others in the workplace and at home as we are welcoming and forgiving in the eucharistic community.

Forming character also takes critical self-appraisal. When our lives get so absorbed by ministerial activities, we can quickly lose touch with our inner selves. Therapy and spiritual direction are certainly two resources to help us come to critical self-awareness. Another means is the practice of examining conscience. We can exercise this practice in a few minutes in a busy schedule, or we can make it a special part of our routine of daily meditation. It is simply the practice of self-remembering that begins by being alone. We call to mind the graces of our day and the attitudes and behaviors that made up our response: "Have I been grateful? Faithful?

Respectful? Selfish? Impetuous? Thoughtful?" When we connect with our inner self and name our blessings, then we can direct certain admonitions inspired by grace to modify our behavior: life is a gift, show more gratitude; don't be so impulsive; slow down and think it through; lighten up a bit; laugh a little more, especially at yourself. As we come to know ourselves, we can affirm our growth and continue to be the person we have come to know, or we can choose a new direction by making a conscious choice to act differently.

Closely related to the examination of conscience, but more extended, is making a retreat. When we decided to enter the ministry, our decision was accompanied by a vision of life and a commitment to become a certain kind of person. Sometimes, that original commitment and vision gets weakened, but not destroyed, through the course of a busy ministry. What remains can be renewed. Retreats are a typical time to make that renewal. By taking time apart, we give ourselves an opportunity for a more thorough examination of where we are heading, how we hope to get there, and who we are becoming.

When engaged with the right intention, spiritual practices like these have the power to form our imagination, emotions, and dispositions so that our experiences of loving God and being loved by God can give rise to moral sensibilities that will extend the range of love's influence on the world.

These four aids along the way help us internalize virtues. The virtues that form the way to goodness and holiness become firm and settled through years of practice. There is no quick and easy substitute for observation, imitation, affirmation, and practice over the long haul. Being formed in virtue is the cumulative effect of many small choices and daily practices that increase our proficiency in the virtues and gradually form our character. But we do not do this alone. Family, friends, mentors, models, the fictional characters we read about and admire as well as the biblical ones, along with the whole community of saints, dead and alive, contribute to the sort of minister we will become. In the end, we make our way to goodness and holiness when we act from virtue—that is, from internalized dispositions that yield actions that feel like they are second nature to us. The confirming sign of goodness and holiness is the sense of harmony and peace we feel and that is confirmed by the community as truly the presence of God's work in our midst.

# Notes

## Chapter 1—pages 3–33

1. Michael Downey, *Understanding Christian Spirituality* (New York: Paulist Press, 1997), 45.

2. James Keenan, "Proposing Cardinal Virtues," *Theological Studies* 56 (December 1995): 709–29.

3. See William C. Spohn, *Go and Do Likewise* (New York: Continuum, 1999), chap. 3.

4. Ibid., 54.

5. The notion that we are to be "faithful" and "creative" to the paradigm of Jesus is influenced by Sandra Schneiders, "Faith, Hermeneutics, and the Literal Sense of Scripture," *Theological Studies* 39 (1978): 731. It is further developed for the moral life by Russell B. Connors Jr., "Music and Morality: 'Performance' and the Normative Claim of Scores and Texts," in *Seeking Goodness and Beauty*, ed. Patricia Lamoureux and Kevin J. O'Neil (Lanham, MD: Rowman and Littlefield, 2005), 147–64.

6. John Shea, *The Restless Widow* (Collegeville, MN: Liturgical Press, 2006), 49–50.

7. On understanding the reign of God using the metaphor "God's dream," see Marcus J. Borg, *The God We Never Knew* (San Francisco: HarperSanFrancisco, 1997), 132–53.

8. On this characteristic of inclusiveness of Jesus in contrast to the other religious personalities and established groups of his day, see Hugo Echegaray, *The Practice of Jesus*, trans. Matthew J. O'Connell (Maryknoll: Orbis Books, 1984), chap. 3, 39–67.

9. On this interpretation, see John Shea, "Jesus' Response to God as Abba: Prayer and Service," in *Contemporary Spirituality: Responding to the Divine Initiative*, ed. Francis A. Eigo (Villanova: The Villanova University Press, 1983), 53.

10. For this interpretation, see ibid., 54.

11. Shea, *The Restless Widow*, 180–81.

12. For this interpretation, see Mary Daniel Turner, "Woman and Power," *The Way Supplement* 53 (Summer 1985): 113–14.

13. Sandra Schneiders, "A Community of Friends (John 13:1-20)," in *Written That You May Believe* (New York: Crossroad, 1999), 162–79, see esp. 172–74.

14. For this interpretation of the passion from the perspective of power, see Donald Senior, "Passion and Resurrection in the Gospel of Mark," *Chicago Studies* 25 (April 1986): 21–34, esp. 25–27.

15. See James Davidson Hunter, *The Death of Character* (New York: Basic Books, 2000), 158–60.

16. Mark Salzman, *Lying Awake* (New York: Alfred A. Knopf, 2000), 172.

17. Spohn, *Go and Do Likewise*, 62.

18. This tripartite structure of virtue ethics is developed by Joseph J. Kotva Jr. in *The Christian Case for Virtue Ethics* (Washington, DC: Georgetown University Press, 1996), 17–20. This structure is used again by James Keenan in his essay "Virtue Ethics" in Bernard Hoose, ed., *Christian Ethics: An Introduction* (London: Cassell, 1998), 84–94.

19. *ST* I, q. 6, ad. 3; *ST* I-II, q. 58, a. 5. On connatural knowledge, see also Karl Rahner, *The Dynamic Element in the Church* (New York: Herder and Herder, 1964), 161ff.; Daniel C. Maguire, "The Knowing Heart and the Intellectualistic Fallacy," in *The Moral Revolution* (San Francisco: Harper & Row, 1986), 259–61; Andrew Tallon, "The Heart in Rahner's Philosophy of Mysticism," *Theological Studies* 53 (December 1992): 711.

20. This theme of judging in the blink of an eye is explored to great effect in the popular book of Malcolm Gladwell, *Blink* (New York: Little, Brown and Company, 2005).

21. Alfred Lansing, *Endurance: Shackleton's Incredible Voyage* (New York: Carroll & Graf Publishers, Inc., 1959), 17.

22. *Nicomachean Ethics*, book II, 1103b.

23. Malcolm Gladwell, *Outliers* (New York: Little, Brown and Company, 2008), 42.

24. *Nicomachean Ethics*, book II, 1105a 30.

25. Ibid., book II, 1105b5-10.

26. Daniel Coyle, *The Talent Code* (New York: Bantam Dell, 2009), see esp. 30–46 for the science of myelination and the process of automaticity that makes skills seem as if we've always possessed them.

27. Ibid., 88.

28. William F. May, "Professional Ethics: Setting, Terrain, and Teacher," in *Ethics Teaching in Higher Education*, ed. Daniel Callahan and Sissela Bok (New York: Plenum Press, 1980), 231.

## Chapter 2—pages 37–65

1. This pattern of the "imitation of God" for the moral life is drawn out more completely by James M. Gustafson, *Can Ethics Be Christian?* (Chicago: University of Chicago Press, 1975), 114–16.

2. Ronald Rolheiser, *The Holy Longing* (New York: Doubleday, 1999), 66.

3. This theme is developed to great effect by Br. David Steindl-Rast in *Gratefulness, the Heart of Prayer* (New York: Paulist Press, 1984), 17ff.

4. Robert A. Emmons and Teresa T. Kneezel, "Giving Thanks: Spiritual and Religious Correlates of Gratitude," *Journal of Psychology and Christianity* 24 (2005): 141.

5. Robert Emmons, *Thanks!* (Boston: Houghton Mifflin Company, 2007), 6.

6. John Shea, *Starlight* (New York: Crossroad, 1993), 83.

7. Gustafson, *Can Ethics Be Christian?* 100.

8. Emmons, *Thanks!* 9.

9. Ibid., 185–209, for ten suggestions on practicing gratitude.

10. John Steinbeck, *East of Eden* (New York: Viking Press, 1952), 130.

11. This the central image of humility in the short analysis of Everett L. Worthington Jr., *Humility: The Quiet Virtue* (Philadelphia: Templeton Foundation Press, 2007).

12. As found in Everett L. Worthington Jr., "Humility: The Quiet Virtue," *Journal of Psychology and Christianity* 27 (2008): 273.

13. David S. Schuller, "Identifying the Criteria for Ministry," in *Ministry in America*, ed. David S. Schuller, Merton P. Strommen, and Milo L. Brekke (San Francisco: Harper and Row, 1980), 19–20. For an elaboration of this trait and others, see Daniel O. Aleshire, "Eleven Major Areas of Ministry," 23–53. A follow-up study in 1987 confirmed this character trait as important for ministry. See Daniel O. Aleshire, "ATS Profiles in Ministry Project," in *Clergy Assessment and Career Development*, ed. Richard A. Hunt, John E. Hinkle Jr., and H. Newton Malony (Nashville: Abingdon Press, 1990), 97–103.

14. On this interpretation of humility as the practice of seeking self-knowledge, see Lisa Fullam, "Humility: A Pilgrim's Virtue," *New Theology Review* 19 (May 2006): 46–53.

15. For James F. Keenan, self-esteem is what makes humility possible. See his *Virtues for Ordinary Christians* (Kansas City: Sheed and Ward, 1996), esp. 71.

16. For a discussion of "normal narcissism" and healthy humility, see Phyllis Zagano, "Spiritual Wisdom, Narcissism, and 'Healthy Humility,'" *The Journal of Pastoral Counseling* 39 (2004): 19–34.

17. Ernest Hemingway, *The Old Man and the Sea* (New York: Simon and Shuster, Inc., Scribner Paperback Fiction, 1995), 110.

18. Viktor Frankl, *Man's Search for Meaning*, trans. Ilse Lasch, rev. ed. (New York: Simon and Shuster, Inc., 1962), 65.

19. John Shea, *The Challenge of Jesus* (Garden City: Doubleday, 1977), 9–113.

20. On the tension between loyalty and truth, see Monika K. Hellwig, *Public Dimensions of a Believer's Life* (Lanham, MD: Rowman & Littlefield Publishers, Inc., 2005), 37–44.

21. Aristotle, *Nicomachean Ethics*, book IX, 1170b9-14. For a succinct overview of Aristotle's notion of character-friendship, see Paul J. Wadell, *Friendship and the Moral Life* (Notre Dame: University of Notre Dame Press, 1989), 46–69. Also, Diana Fritz Cates, "Spending the Day with a Good Friend: Autobiography, Moral Character, and the Religious Imagination," in *Seeking Goodness and Beauty: The Use of the Arts in Theological Ethics*, ed. Patricia Lamoureux and Kevin J. O'Neil (Lanham, MD: Rowman & Littlefield Publishers, Inc., 2005), 35–40.

22. Paul J. Wadell, *Becoming Friends* (Grand Rapids: Brazos Press, 2002).

23. For an analysis of the dynamics of love in this movie, see Patricia A. Lamoureux, "The Transformative Power of Love in *Shadowlands*," in Lamoureux and O'Neil, eds., *Seeking Goodness and Beauty*, 71–86.

24. Aristotle, *Nicomachean Ethics*, book VIII, 1155a5.

25. For an excellent treatment of various ways to understand self-referent love, see Edward C. Vacek, *Love, Human and Divine: The Heart of Christian Ethics* (Washington, DC: Georgetown University Press, 1994), see esp. 198–279.

26. Edward J. Farrell, *The Father Is Very Fond of Me* (Denville, NJ: Dimension Books, Inc., 1975), 5.

27. Some very helpful and accessible insights into the dynamics of acquiring healthy self-esteem can be found in Robert J. Wicks, *Touching the Holy* (Notre Dame: Ave Maria Press, 1993), 61–89.

## Chapter 3—pages 66–87

1. Marcus Borg speaks of Jesus as "spirit person" in his *Meeting Jesus for the First Time* (San Francisco: HarperSanFrancisco, 1995), 31–39.

2. Emotional intelligence, simply put, is the ability to access our own feelings, to distinguish them, and to draw upon them to guide our behavior. A detailed description of emotional intelligence is in Daniel Goleman, *Emotional Intelligence* (New York: Bantam Books, 1995), 42–44.

3. A helpful guide to the process of discernment through its various ways of knowing is Elizabeth Liebert, *The Way of Discernment* (Louisville: Westminster John Knox Press, 2008).

4. Arthur Miller, *Death of a Salesman*, in *The Portable Arthur Miller*, ed. Harold Clurman (New York: Viking Press, 1971), 50.

5. On the "dream of God" as an interpretation of the reign of God, see Marcus Borg, *The God We Never Knew* (San Francisco: HarperSanFrancisco, 1998),132–53. On integrating outward listening to inward listening, see John Neafsey, *A Sacred Voice is Calling* (Maryknoll: Orbis Books, 2006).

6. William C. Spohn, *Go and Do Likewise: Jesus and Ethics* (New York: Continuum, 1999), 152–53.

7. On this important spiritual discipline for holiness, see Robert Ellsberg, *The Saints' Guide to Holiness* (New York: North Point Press, 2003), 59–78.

8. Edward Vacek, *Love, Human and Divine: The Heart of Christian Ethics* (Washington, DC: Georgetown University Press, 1994), 141–46.

9. On piety as a virtue, see James Gustafson, "Say Something Theological," 1981 Ryerson Lecture at the University of Chicago, pp. 5–7; see also Mark Allan Powell, *Loving Jesus* (Minneapolis: Fortress Press, 2004): 18–22.

10. Spohn, *Jesus and Ethics*, 14.

11. On the requirement of a sense of the normal as basic to perceiving incongruity, see Robert C. Roberts, "Sense of Humor as a Christian Virtue," *Faith and Philosophy* 7 (April 1990): 181.

12. See, for example, the studies reviewed by Donald Capps and his response to them in Donald Capps, "Religion and Humor: Estranged Bedfellows," *Pastoral Psychology* 54 (May 2006): 413–38. See also a response to the argument that humor is incompatible with Christianity in Robert C. Roberts, "Smiling with God: Reflections on Christianity and the Psychology of Humor," *Faith and Philosophy* 4 (April 1987): 168–75.

13. Umberto Eco, *The Name of the Rose* (New York: Harcourt, Brace, Jovanovich, 1983).

14. Norman Cousins, *Anatomy of an Illness* (New York: Bantam Books, 1979), 39–40.

15. Ibid., 145–46.

16. Donald Capps, "The Psychological Benefits of Humor," *Pastoral Psychology* 54 (May 2006): 393–411.

17. Peter L. Berger, *A Rumor of Angels* (Garden City: Doubleday, 1969), 86–94, where he develops the notion of humor along with four other "signals of transcendence—order, play, hope, and damnation. See also, his *Redeeming Laughter* (New York: Walter de Gruyter & Co., 1997), see esp. 205–15.

18. On humor and perspective, see Roberts, "Sense of Humor as a Christian Virtue," 180–84.

19. Doris Donnelly ends her essay with nine suggestions to revitalize our sense of humor. See "Divine Folly: Being Religious and the Exercise of Humor," *Theology Today* 48 (January 1992): 397–98.

## Chapter 4—pages 88–105

1. Louis J. Cameli, "Do You Need to Be Smart to Be a Priest Today? Meeting the Intellectual Imperative," *Seminary Journal* 12 (Winter 2006): 45–46.

2. Bernard Lonergan, "Cognitional Structure," in *Collection*, ed. F. E. Crowe (New York: Herder and Herder, 1967), 221–39.

3. Simone Weil, "Reflections on the Right Use of School Studies," in *Waiting for God*, trans. Emma Craufurd (New York: G.P. Putnam's Sons, 1951), 105–16.

4. For an excellent reflection on reading as a spiritual practice, see Stephanie Paulsell, "'The Inscribed Heart: A Spirituality of Intellectual Work': Reading as a Spiritual Practice," *Lexington Theological Quarterly* 36 (Fall 2001): 139–54. See

also her "Spiritual Formation and Intellectual Work in Theological Education," *Theology Today* 55 (July 1998): 229–34.

5. For two very accessible treatments of prudence, see Raymond Devettere, *Introduction to Virtue Ethics* (Washington, DC: Georgetown University Press, 2002), 87–138; and Paul J. Wadell, *Happiness and the Christian Moral Life* (Lanham, MD: Rowman & Littlefield, 2008), 182–91. For a more detailed treatment of prudence in Aquinas, see the close reading of appropriate texts in Daniel Mark Nelson, *The Priority of Prudence* (University Park: The Pennsylvania State University Press, 1992), see esp. 69–104.

6. Aristotle, *Nicomachean Ethics*, 1094b 13-15.

7. *ST* I-II, q. 94, a.4.

8. *ST* I-II, qq. 47-52.

9. Aristotle, *Nicomachean Ethics*, 1142a 12-15.

10. *ST* I-II, q.18, a.3. This quote must be understood within the larger context of Aquinas's teaching that the morality of the act comes from the object of the act.

11. *ST* I-II, q. 7, a. 3. A very helpful commentary on these reality-revealing questions can be found in Daniel C. Maguire, *The Moral Choice* (Garden City: Doubleday, 1978), 128–88.

## Chapter 5—pages 106–144

1. Daniel C. Maguire, *A New American Justice* (Garden City: Doubleday, 1980), 58.

2. Ibid., 57.

3. Paul J. Wadell, *The Moral of the Story* (New York: The Crossroad Publishing Co., 2002), 134.

4. The notion of the common good is a rich social concept in the Catholic tradition. An outstanding, but extensive, analysis can be found in David Hollenbach, *The Common Good and Christian Ethics* (Cambridge: Cambridge University Press, 2002). Shorter and more accessible treatments of this notion can be found in Michael J. Himes and Kenneth R. Himes, *Fullness of Faith* (New York: Paulist Press, 1993), 39–54; see also, Maguire, *A New American Justice*, 85–98.

5. This threefold movement is more fully developed in Fred Kammer, *Doing Faithjustice: An Introduction to Catholic Social Thought* (New York: Paulist Press, 1991), 147–59. This book is a valuable resource to explore further the themes of this virtue.

6. Wadell, *The Moral of the Story*, 134.

7. As found in Paul J. Wharton, *Stories and Parables for Preachers and Teachers* (New York: Paulist Press, 1986), 26.

8. Recall here the often quoted line from the ending of the introduction to the 1971 synodal document, *Justice in the World*: "Action on behalf of justice and participation in the transformation of the world fully appear to us as a constitutive

dimension of the preaching of the Gospel, or in other words, of the Church's mission for the redemption of the human race and its liberation from every oppressive situation."

9. Johann Baptist Metz, *The Emergent Church*, trans. Peter Mann (New York: Crossroad, 1981), 35.

10. Elizabeth A. Johnson, *She Who Is* (New York: Crossroad, 1992), see esp. 179–85, 266–69.

11. Martha C. Nussbaum, *Upheavals of Thought: The Intelligence of Emotions* (New York: Cambridge University Press, 2001), 319.

12. Ibid., 302.

13. Ibid., 301–2.

14. As found in Robert Coles, *The Moral Intelligence of Children* (New York: Random House, 1997), 10–11.

15. For a review of this research, see Sidney Callahan, *In Good Conscience* (New York: HarperCollins, 1991), 186–90; also, Charles Shelton, *Morality of the Heart: A Psychology of the Christian Moral Life* (New York: Crossroad, 1990), 124–39.

16. Harper Lee, *To Kill a Mockingbird* (New York: Warner Books, Inc., 1960), 30.

17. Eric J. Cassell, *The Nature of Suffering* (New York: Oxford University Press, 1991), 30–47.

18. James F. Keenan, *Moral Wisdom* (Lanham, MD: Rowman & Littlefield, 2004), 68–69.

19. Stanley Hauerwas, *Naming the Silences* (Grand Rapids, MI: William B. Eerdmans, 1990), 53.

20. Daniel Callahan, *The Troubled Dream of Life* (Washington, DC: Georgetown University Press, 2002), 96–97.

21. On the social dimension of compassion, see Marcus J. Borg, *The God We Never Knew* (New York: HarperCollins Publishers, 1997), 149–53.

22. For an excellent treatment of the vice of greed in the moral tradition, see Rebecca Konyndyk DeYoung, *Glittering Vices* (Grand Rapids, MI: Brazos Press, 2009), 99–116.

23. See http://www.payitforwardmovement.org/.

24. *Nicomachean Ethics*, book III, 1115a 30.

25. *ST*, II-II, q. 124, aa. 2, 3. For a close reading of the various aspects of courage according to Aquinas, see Lee H. Yearley, *Mencius and Aquinas: Theories of Virtue and Conceptions of Courage* (Albany: State University of New York Press, 1990), 113–43.

26. Harper Lee, *To Kill a Mockingbird* (New York: Warner Books, 1960), 112.

27. Ibid., 105.

28. These are the three elements of courage that Rushworth M. Kidder uses to structure his book, *Moral Courage* (New York: William Morrow, 2005).

29. As adapted from the John Wayne reference in ibid., 9.

30. Josef Pieper, *The Four Cardinal Virtues* (Notre Dame: University of Notre Dame Press, 1966), 126.

31. As found in ibid., 137.

32. *ST*, II-II, q. 123, 2.

33. For an excellent analysis of how to practice courage, see Katherine Platt, "Gut Is a Habit: The Practice of Courage," in *Courage*, ed. Barbara Darling-Smith (Notre Dame: University of Notre Dame Press, 2002), 132–46.

## Chapter 6—pages 147–161

1. Daniel Mark Nelson, *The Priority of Prudence* (University Park: The Pennsylvania State University Press, 1992), 142.

2. On a review of some of the social-psychological literature on the influence of groups on an individual's values, see Timothy E. O'Connell, *Making Disciples* (New York: Crossroad, 1998), esp. 75–86.

3. James Davidson Hunter, *The Death of Character* (New York: Basic Books, 2000), 163.

4. For this understanding of culture, see Robert Bellah, et al., *Habits of the Heart* (Berkeley: University of California Press, 1985), 333.

5. Paul J. Wadell has given an extensive analysis of friendship for moral formation in *Friendship and the Moral Life* (Notre Dame: The University of Notre Dame Press, 1989); and in *Becoming Friends* (Grand Rapids, MI: Brazos Press, 2002). See also the short essay by Joseph Kotva Jr., "Seeking Out Good Friends," in *Practice What You Preach*, ed. James F. Keenan and Joseph Kotva Jr. (Franklin, WI: Sheed and Ward, 1999), 71–80.

6. On types of friends for ministry, see Robert J. Wicks, *Touching the Holy* (Notre Dame: Ave Maria Press, 1992), 93–122.

7. Ibid., 102.

8. Timothy O'Connell has provided a helpful analysis of the role of mentors and models in moral formation in *Making Disciples* (New York: Crossroad 1998), 87–94.

9. Robert Coles, *The Moral Intelligence of Children* (New York: Random House, 1997), 5–6.

10. On appealing to the paradigmatic individual, see Harold Alderman, "By Virtue of a Virtue" in *Virtue Ethics: A Critical Reader*, ed. Daniel Statman (Washington, DC: Georgetown University Press, 1997), 145–64.

11. On this notion of moving imaginatively from the story of Jesus to the present situation by analogical reasoning, see William C. Spohn, *Go and Do Likewise* (New York: Continuum, 1999), 50–71.

12. Ibid., 14.

13. Joseph Kotva Jr., "Transformed in Prayer," in Keenan and Kotva, *Practice What You Preach*, 147–56.

14. Paul J. Wadell, "What Do All Those Masses Do for Us?" in *Living No Longer for Ourselves*, ed. Kathleen Hughes and Mark R. Francis (Collegeville, MN: Liturgical Press, 1991), 153–69.